I0752984

MYPHOTOWALK

THE POWER OF THE GOSPEL

CATHERINE MARTIN

MYPHOTOWALK

THE POWER OF THE GOSPEL

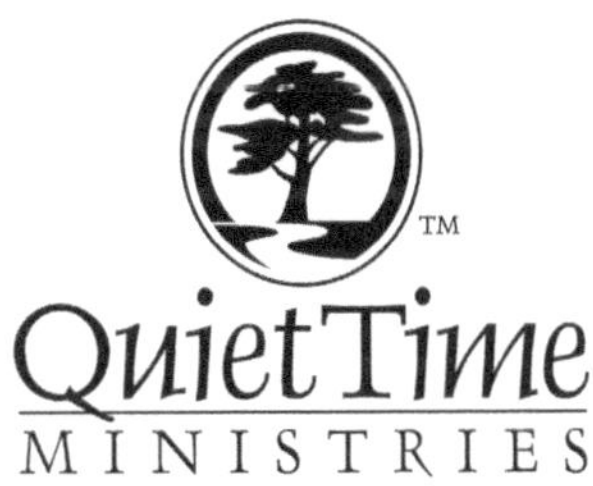

Quiet Time Ministries
PALM DESERT, CALIFORNIA

Cover by Quiet Time Ministries.
Cover photo by Catherine Martin—myPhotoWalk.com

Interior photos by Catherine Martin available at MYPHOTOWALK.COM—CATHERINEMARTIN.SMUGMUG.COM

myPhotoWalk—The Power Of The Gospel

Published by Quiet Time Ministries
Palm Desert, California 92255
www.quiettime.org

ISBN-13: 978-1-7375747-1-2

Printed in the United States of America

25 26 27 28 29 30 31 32 33 / LSI / 10 9 8 7 6 5 4 3 2 1

To my Lord and Savior Jesus Christ, The Lover of my soul,
Redeemer, Savior, Good Shepherd, King of kings, Lord of lords,
Light of the World, Alpha and Omega, Bright Morning Star,
Prince of Peace, Wonderful Counselor, and the Author and Perfecter of my faith.
"Overwhelming victory is ours through Christ, who loved us."

Romans 8:37 NLT

To my beloved husband, David G. Martin, M.D.
who has been my joy and delight for more than 40 years.
Thank you for your tireless and loving work in Quiet Time Ministries.

To those who partner with me in Quiet Time Ministries
teaching devotion to God and His Word
to men and women throughout the world.

To those who study God's Word together with me throughout the world
in our online Bible studies and in groups that use our quiet time studies.

May we all fix our eyes on Jesus the champion of our faith
and fall before Him in loving adoration and worship as
we take a journey into our life in Jesus Christ
and discover *the power of the gospel.*

Books by Catherine Martin

Six Secrets to a Powerful Quiet Time — A 30-Day Journey ©2005, 2014

Knowing and Loving the Bible — A 30-Day Journey ©2007

Walking with the God Who Cares — A 30-Day Journey ©2007, 2016

Set My Heart on Fire — A 30-Day Journey ©2008

Trusting in the Names of God — A 30-Day Journey ©2008, A Quiet Time Experience ©2008, 2015

Passionate Prayer — A 30-Day Journey ©2009, A Quiet Time Experience ©2009

Pilgrimage of the Heart — Quiet Times for the Heart ©2003, 2016

Revive my Heart — Quiet Times for the Heart ©2003, 2011

A Heart that Dances — Quiet Times for the Heart ©2003, 2022

A Heart on Fire — Quiet Times for the Heart ©2002, 2012

A Heart to See Forever — Quiet Times for the Heart ©2003, 2011

A Heart that Hopes in God — A Quiet Time Experience ©2007, 2011

Run Before the Wind — A Quiet Time Experience ©2008, 2012

Walk on Water Faith — A Quiet Time Experience ©2014

One Holy Passion — A Quiet Time Experience ©2017

The Proof of God's Amazing Love — A Quiet Time Experience ©2024

A Woman's Heart that Dances — A Devotional Journey ©2009

A Woman's Walk in Grace — A Devotional Journey ©2010

The Calling — A Devotional Journey ©2019

Quiet Time Moments for Women — A 366-Day Devotional ©2025

The Quiet Time Notebook & The Quiet Time Journal — A Quiet Time Notebooks ©1994, 2012-2013

The Devotional Bible Study Notebook — A Quiet Time Notebook ©2010, 2013

The Passionate Prayer Notebook — A Quiet Time Notebook ©2013

myPhotoWalk—Quiet Time Moments — Devotional Photography ©2016

myPhotoWalk—Savoring God's Promises of Hope — Devotional Photography ©2017

myPhotoWalk—The Story of Your Life — Devotional Photography ©2020

myPhotoWalk—A Day in the Life of God — Devotional Photography ©2023

Contents

Experiencing Life In Christ

A persistent knock on the door of my one room apartment at Arizona State University forced me to get up from my desk chair and answer. I opened the door to see a young preppy couple with welcoming smiles. I smiled back. "Hello, what can I do for *you*?" Little did I realize they were actually there to do something for *me*! They shared their names and then said, "We're visiting students here at ASU to ask if you have ever heard about having a relationship with God?"

That's not something you hear every day. "Well, my mother raised us to know God," I replied, "... and, uh...I went to church sometimes." *Where was this conversation going?*

"We would love to share a booklet with you that talks about four spiritual laws and explains all about knowing God. Could we share that with you?" They smiled again.

Hesitantly, yet interested—I don't know why—I invited the couple in.

We sat down at the kitchen table and they began reading from the yellow booklet. The laws went something like this:

- Law 1: God loves you and has a wonderful plan for your life.
- Law 2: Sin has separated us from God so that we cannot know God's love or plan for our lives.
- Law 3: Jesus Christ is God's provision for our sin. Jesus said in John 14:6 of the Bible —"I am the way, and the truth, and the life; no one comes to the Father but through Me."
- Law 4: We must receive Christ into our lives so that we can know God's love and plan for our lives.

To be honest, they had my attention at Law 3. *I am the way, and the truth, and the life; no one comes to the Father but through Me.* That verse began spinning around in my head, Where did that come from?

I suddenly realized I was just sitting there with my mouth open not saying anything. The couple stared right back, then picked up the pace. "Would you like to pray to receive Christ and experience new life in Him—and a relationship with God?" Well, that scared me to the core, I can tell you. I'm not one to jump into things and I certainly wasn't about to pray a prayer willy-nilly without thinking through everything. So I cleared my throat and said haltingly, "I'll think about it." The couple exchanged glances. They prayed for me, left the booklet, and got up to leave. As they walked out the door, they turned back and encouraged, "Catherine, we'll be praying for you." They meant it!

So for the next six months, I went about my life studying and partying with my friends. After all, I was only eighteen, and this was college! But—and this is the strangest thing—I could not get the words of Jesus out of my mind and thoughts. John 14:6, John 14:6, John 14:6. "I am the way, and the truth, and the life." "THE WAY" "THE TRUTH" "THE LIFE" "No one comes to the Father but through Me." "NO ONE." The words would ring clear in my mind when I would least expect it.

There was this particular time—I'll never forget it—when I went with some friends to our favorite restaurant where we would gather and party after a week of classes and study. I won't go into the details, but, suffice it to say, I got back to my apartment really late—REALLY LATE—and slept for only a few hours. The next morning, I lay in bed thinking, *My life is a waste. I'm going nowhere. I have no purpose.* I was so discouraged I began to despair of life itself.

And then, I heard the John 14:6 words of Jesus spoken softly in my mind—not an actual voice mind you, no celestial choir, no heavenly lights—merely a quiet remembrance of a past thought as if to tell me what my greatest need was and answer all my questions in life. "I am the way, and the truth, and the life; no one comes to the Father but through Me."

I said to a God I really didn't know, *Okay Lord, I'm going to deal with this verse and figure out how it can possibly help me.* I thought through what Jesus was saying. *If Jesus is the way to God, then to follow and live for anything but Him, is to go the wrong way. If He is the truth, then to live for anything else is to live for a lie. And if He is the life, then anything else is not going to give me life.* The truth of Jesus was so very clear to me. It was as though His Presence filled the room and He was meeting with me personally. He was inviting me to give my life to Him. He seemed to be saying to me, "Catherine, it's time you give your life to Me."

Well, you don't have to tell me twice. I immediately got out of bed, got on my knees, and prayed that prayer as I remembered it from the little booklet: *Lord Jesus, I need You. Thank You for dying on the cross for my sins. I ask You now to come into my life, forgive my sins, give me the gift of eternal life, and make me the person You want me to be. Amen.*

I will never forget that morning. That one decision altered the course of my entire life. My life moved from a journey to an adventure, the great adventure of knowing God. I began the glorious experience of life in Jesus Christ. What happened to me is *the power of the gospel.* It's why Paul could say in Romans 1:16—"I am not ashamed of the gospel, for it is the power of God for salvation to everyone who believes, to the Jew first and also to the Greek."

Maybe you have wondered, just like I did, what it means to become a Christian. What is your life in Jesus Christ all about? Or perhaps you are a Christian, but you would like to become closer to God.

What actually happens when we experience salvation in Christ? The best answer I can give is, "A lot more than you can possibly imagine." In my book, *The Proof of God's Amazing Love,* a quiet time study in Paul's letter to the Romans, we experience the real power of the gospel, not only to save, but also to sanctify, grow us spiritually through the work of the Holy Spirit, and set us on the journey of serving our Lord as we live out our days on earth.

When you experience the love of God firsthand in coming face to face with the Lord Jesus Christ, your life will never be the same. In *The Power of the Gospel,* you will discover reflections from Romans and devotional reading from many authors I first shared in *The Proof of God's Amazing Love* to display the neverending benefits and results of the gospel, the "good news of Jesus Christ." One of the great results is an eternal relationship with Jesus Christ as He lives in us through the indwelling Holy Spirit. We are united with Him forever. William Newell (Harvard Divinity School

1829) says it well: "To be joined in life with the Risen Christ, and thus daily, hourly, to walk is a wonder and the blessed portion of all true Christians."

So then, dear friend, as you read and meditate on these reflections from Paul's letter to the Romans, I invite you to drink in their truths, gaze long at God's handiwork in His creation as seen in my devotional photography, and experience anew a powerful and transformative life in Jesus Christ. He is altogether lovely and will walk with you and talk with you all along life's narrow way. God bless you.

In His love,

Catherine Martin

“For I am not ashamed of the gospel,
for it is the power of God for salvation
to everyone who believes,
to the Jew first and also to the Greek.”

Romans 1:16

To be joined in life with the Risen Christ, and thus daily, hourly, to walk is a wonder and the blessed portion of all true Christians.

William Newell

“For to me, to live is Christ and to die is gain.”

Philippians 1:21

He lives, He lives, Christ Jesus lives today
He walks with me and talks with me along life’s narrow way
He lives, He lives, Salvation to impart
You ask me how I know He lives? He lives within my heart.

Alfred H. Ackley

GOSPEL

The gospel is the good news of Jesus Christ. The Apostle Paul proclaimed the gospel and was not ashamed of it. He loved it, preached it, and never stepped away from it. Romans 1:16 declares that the gospel is "the power of God for salvation to everyone who believes..." The gospel reveals our need for God's righteousness, Christ's death on the cross as atonement for our sins, and the road to salvation including justification, redemption, and reconciliation. Experience the gospel's power as you are saved, sanctified, glorified, and enjoying your life in Jesus Christ forever and ever.

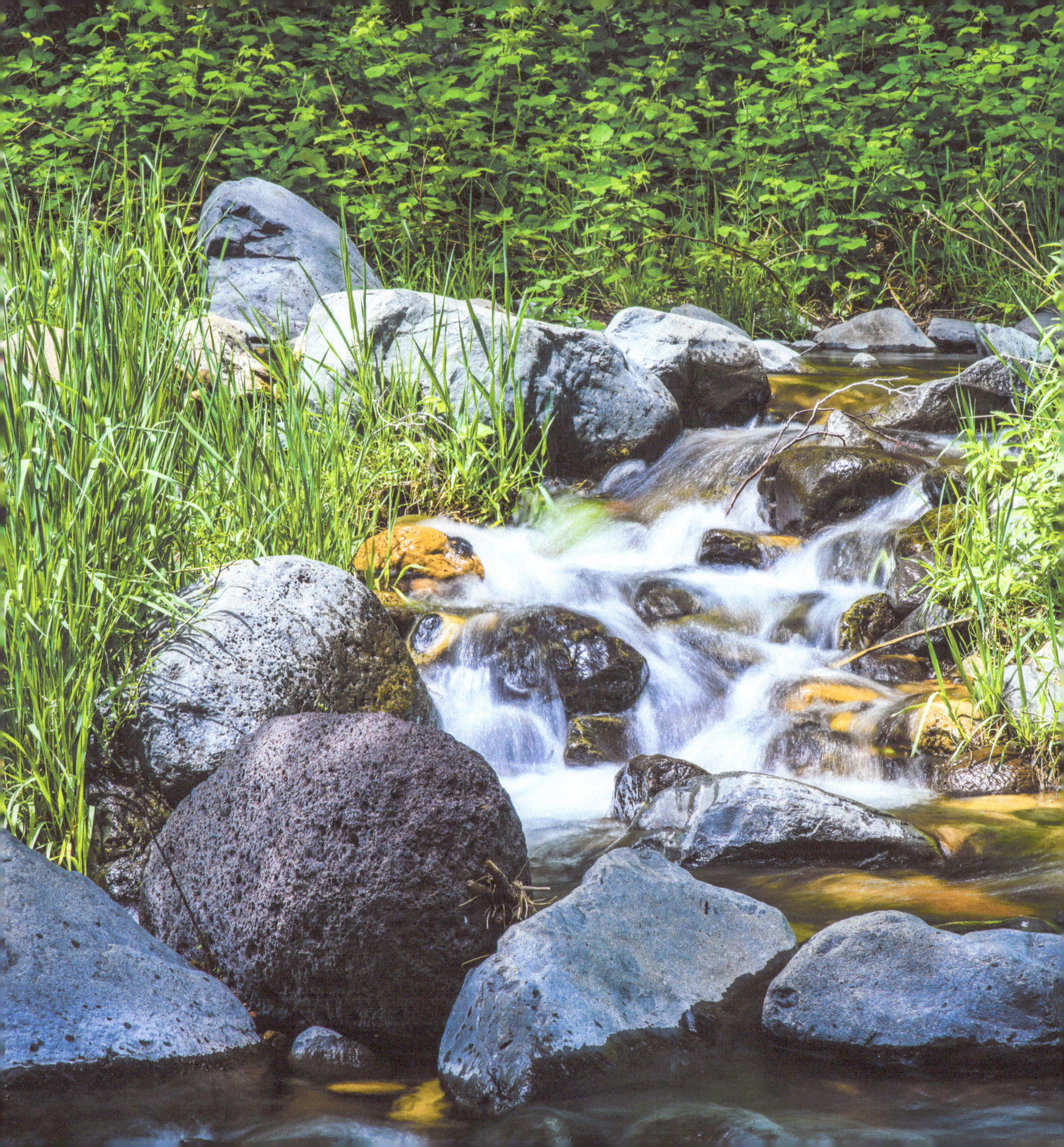

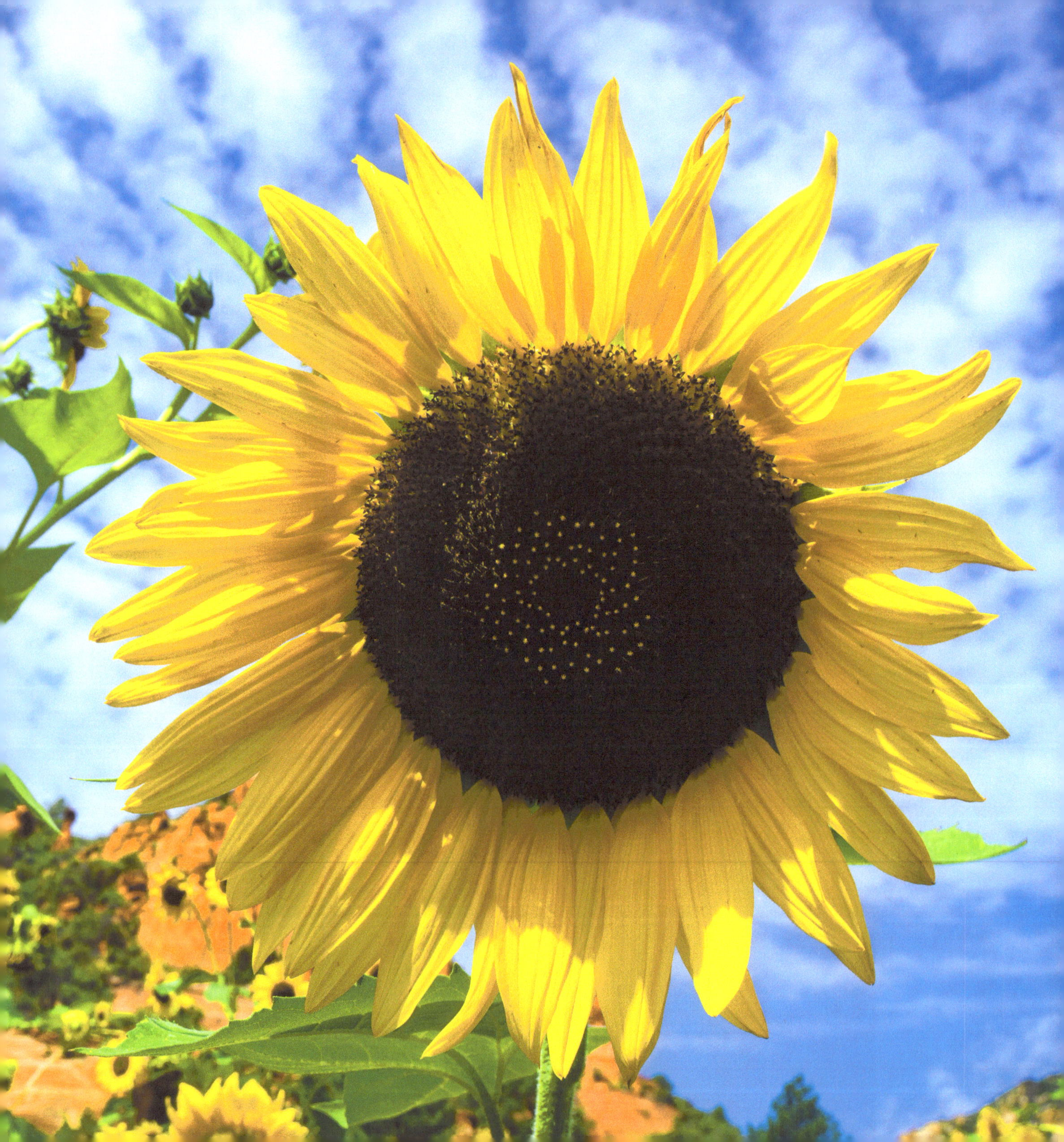

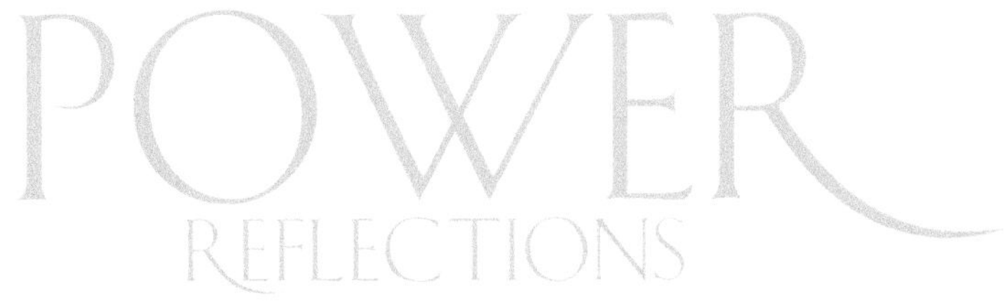

EXPERIENCE GOD'S AMAZING POWER

For I am not ashamed of the gospel, for it is the power of God…
ROMANS 1:16

How is it that everyday people can achieve abundantly more than they thought even possible? Only one way—through the power of the indwelling Holy Spirit, given at the very moment of salvation when a man or woman places their faith in Jesus Christ. Once saved, the power of God is now present and working in you. The word translated "power" in the Greek is *dunamis* and means strength and power that makes you able and capable. Embrace the power of God experienced in the gospel of Jesus Christ now at work in you through the Holy Spirit with continuing results day by day and moment by moment.

Lord, thank You for Your power seen and experienced in the gospel.
Thank You for saving me and working in me now through the power of the Holy Spirit.
I ask You to do a mighty work in and through me. In Jesus' name, Amen.

Blessed are You, O LORD God of Israel our father,
forever and ever. Yours, O LORD, is the greatness and the power
and the glory and the victory and the majesty,
indeed everything that is in the heavens and the earth;
Yours is the dominion, O LORD, and You exalt Yourself as head over all.
Both riches and honor come from You, and You rule over all,
and in Your hand is power and might; and it lies in
Your hand to make great and to strengthen everyone.
Now therefore, our God, we
thank You, and praise Your glorious name.

1 Chronicles 29:10-13

I want to know Christ and experience the mighty power that raised Him from the dead.

Philippians 3:10 nlt

When we understand the sovereignty, power, design, majesty, precision, genius, intimacy, and caring of an Almighty God, it takes away our fear. It removes our frustration. It allows us to sleep at night and trust Him with the running of His own universe. It allows us to have margin. It allows us to resume our proper role in the order of things rather than taking over His role…The more we understand about God's power the less we worry about our weakness.

More Than Meets The Eye — Richard A. Swenson, M.D.

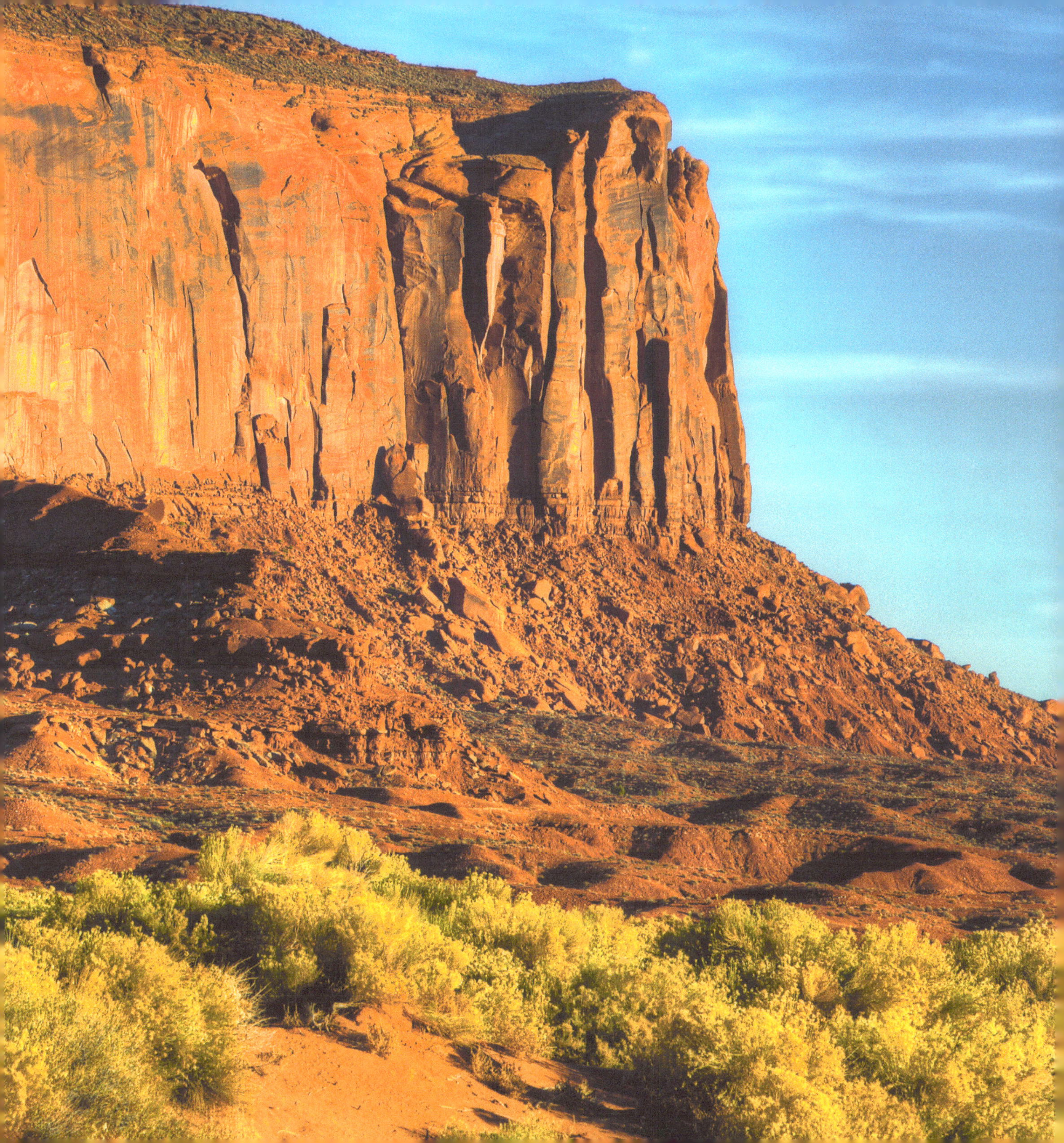

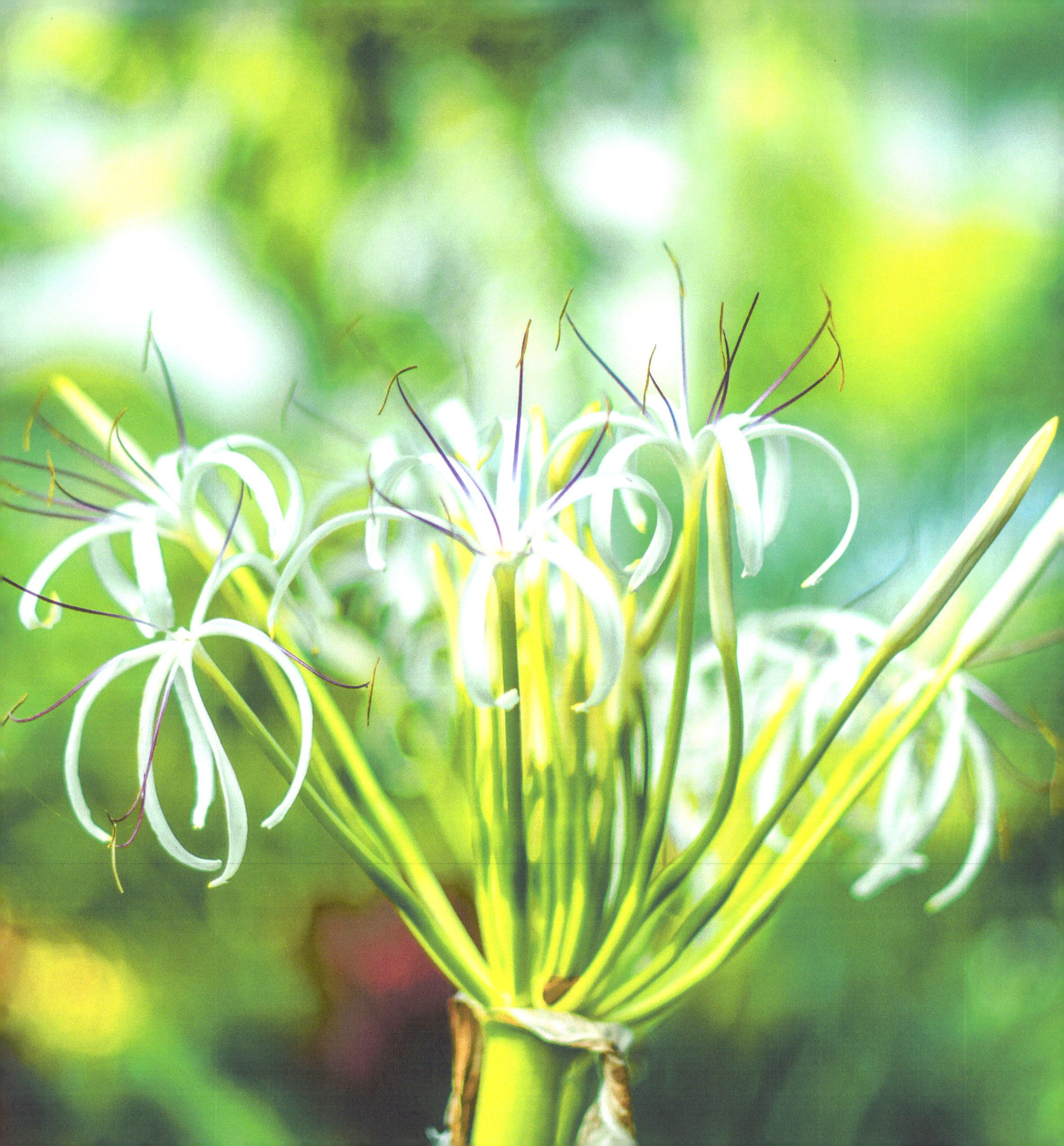

SALVATION
REFLECTIONS

You Can Be Saved

For I am not ashamed of the gospel, for it is the power of God for salvation to everyone who believes...
Romans 1:16

How is a sinful man made right before a holy God? The righteousness of God is a gift of grace for sinners, not a reward for works. Salvation is given by grace through faith as one trusts in the finished work of Christ on the cross. The gospel is good news because in it we learn that we can be saved because Christ did for us what we can never do for ourselves. Oh, how we need salvation if we have not yet placed our faith in Christ—the Greek word translated "salvation" is *soteria* and means safety, deliverance, and preservation from danger or destruction. Jesus has set us free from the slavery of sin and death. He is your Rescuer and Redeemer.

Lord, thank You for the good news that I can be saved and set free from sin and death. I place my faith in You and thank You for dying on the cross for my sins. You are my Rescuer and my Redeemer. In Jesus' name, Amen.

Salvation is entirely and altogether of God, and is the result of the great and eternal love of God...Before the foundation of the world, before the world was ever made, before man was ever created, before time had ever come into existence, God planned this mighty and glorious way of salvation. He planned it in detail; He planned that at a given point in time His Son should come into the world in order to make the Atonement, whereby alone salvation would be made possible...God had planned it all before the foundation of the world...There is no greater proof of the love of God towards us than the fact that He was aware of us, and had chosen us, before the foundation of the world. It was planned that Christ should die for us before we ever lived.

Romans, Exposition of Chapter 5, Assurance — D. Martyn Lloyd-Jones

But God has not destined us for wrath, but for obtaining salvation
through our Lord Jesus Christ.

1 Thessalonians 5:9

An illustration that helps us understand salvation involves a young man who was convicted of a capital offense. He stood before the judge to hear his sentence. The judge read the man's offenses, declared him guilty as charged, and then levied the death penalty. The man stood in front of the judge with great shame and despair. But then there was a shocking and unexpected turn of events. The judge stood, removed his robes, stepped down, and walked over to the prisoner. He turned to the bailiff and said, "I will take this man's place and pay his penalty." Then he told the young man he was free to go. Of course, in real life this would never happen. But for you, dear friend, this act of grace and mercy has happened. The Lord has stepped in and taken your place, atoned for your sins by dying on the cross, and has paid the penalty for you.

The Proof of God's Amazing Love — Catherine Martin

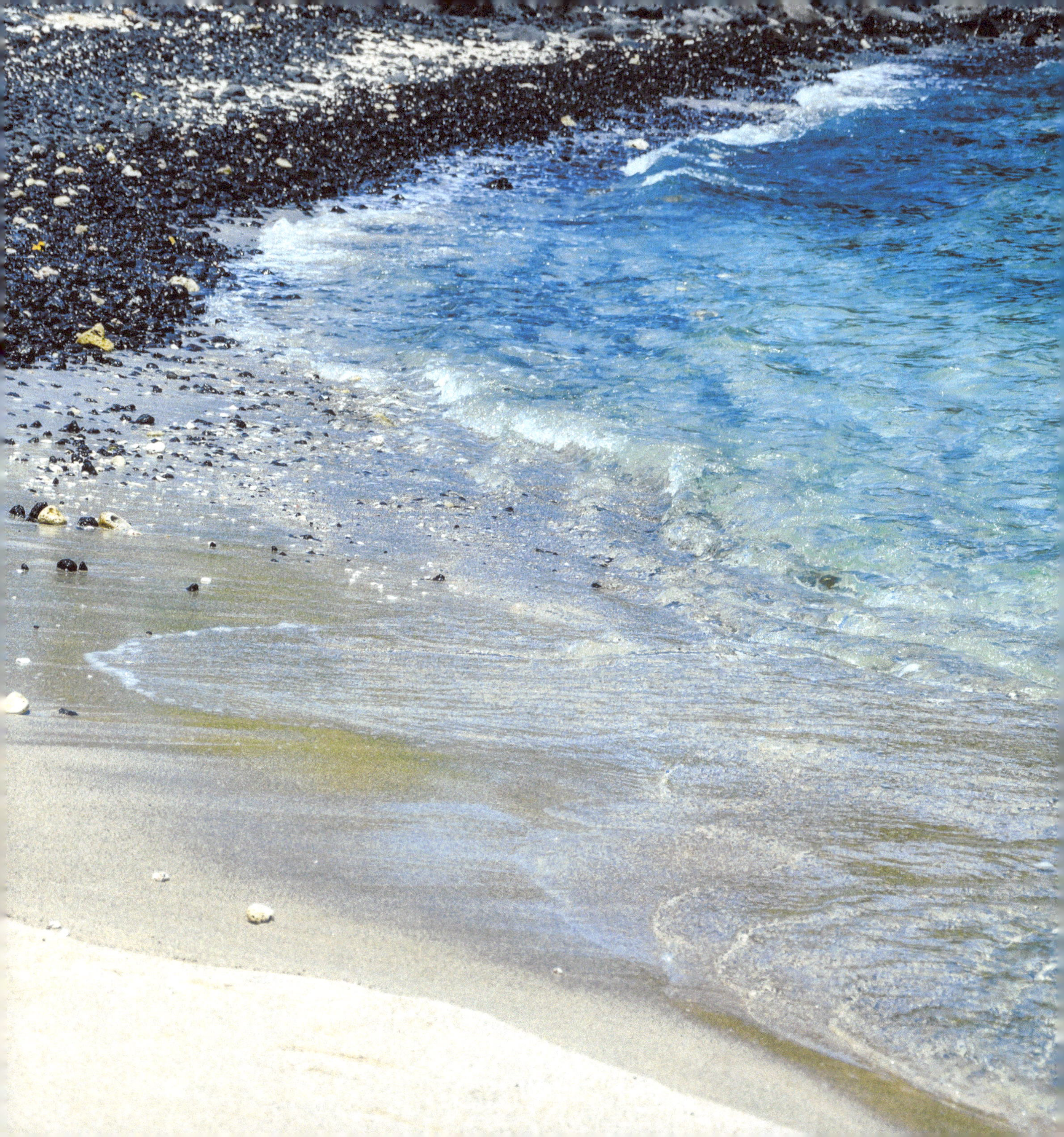

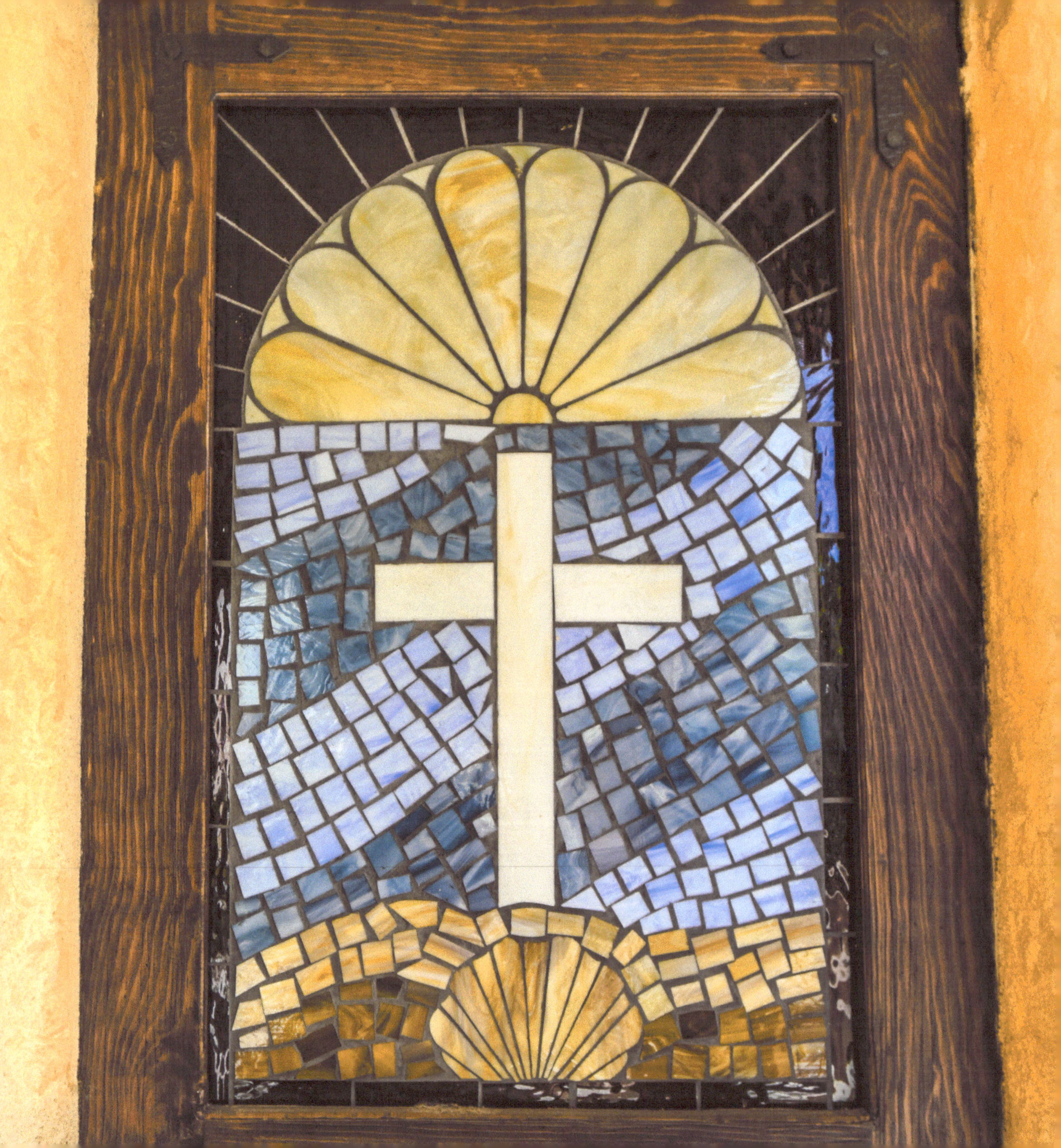

SAVIOR
REFLECTIONS

You Have a Savior

The righteousness of God through faith in Jesus Christ
for all those who believe.
Romans 3:22

Jesus Christ is your Savior and you are His beloved. He died in your place that you might be set free. Hallelujah, what a Savior! Near the end of his life, Philip Paul Bliss wrote a powerful hymn, "Hallelujah, What A Savior." A few weeks before Bliss went home to be with the Lord, he preached a message at the Indiana state prison on "Man of Sorrows," and followed it up with the hymn he had written about his Savior, Jesus Christ. Many prisoners gave their lives to Jesus Christ that day. Do you know the Lord Jesus Christ and love Him today? Tell Him from your heart those wonderful words, "Hallelujah, What A Savior!"

Lord, thank You for setting Your love on me and dying in my place that I may be set free.
You are my beloved Savior. I give my life anew to You and say,
Hallelujah, what a Savior! In Jesus' name, Amen.

Man of Sorrows! What a name; For the Son of God, who came;
Ruined sinners to reclaim. Hallelujah! What a Savior!

Bearing shame and scoffing rude, in my place condemned He stood;
Sealed my pardon with His blood. Hallelujah! What a Savior!

Guilty, vile, and helpless we; Spotless Lamb of God was He;
"Full atonement!" Can it be? Hallelujah! What a Savior!

Lifted up was He to die; "It is finished!" was His cry;
Now in Heav'n exalted high. Hallelujah! What a Savior!

When He comes, our glorious King, all His ransomed home to bring,
Then anew His song we'll sing: Hallelujah! What a Savior!

Hallelujah What a Savior — Philip Paul Bliss

Who has saved us and called us with a holy calling, not according to our works,
but according to His own purpose and grace which was granted us in Christ Jesus
from all eternity, but now has been revealed by the appearing of our Savior Christ Jesus,
who abolished death and brought life and immortality to light through the gospel.

2 Timothy 1:9-10

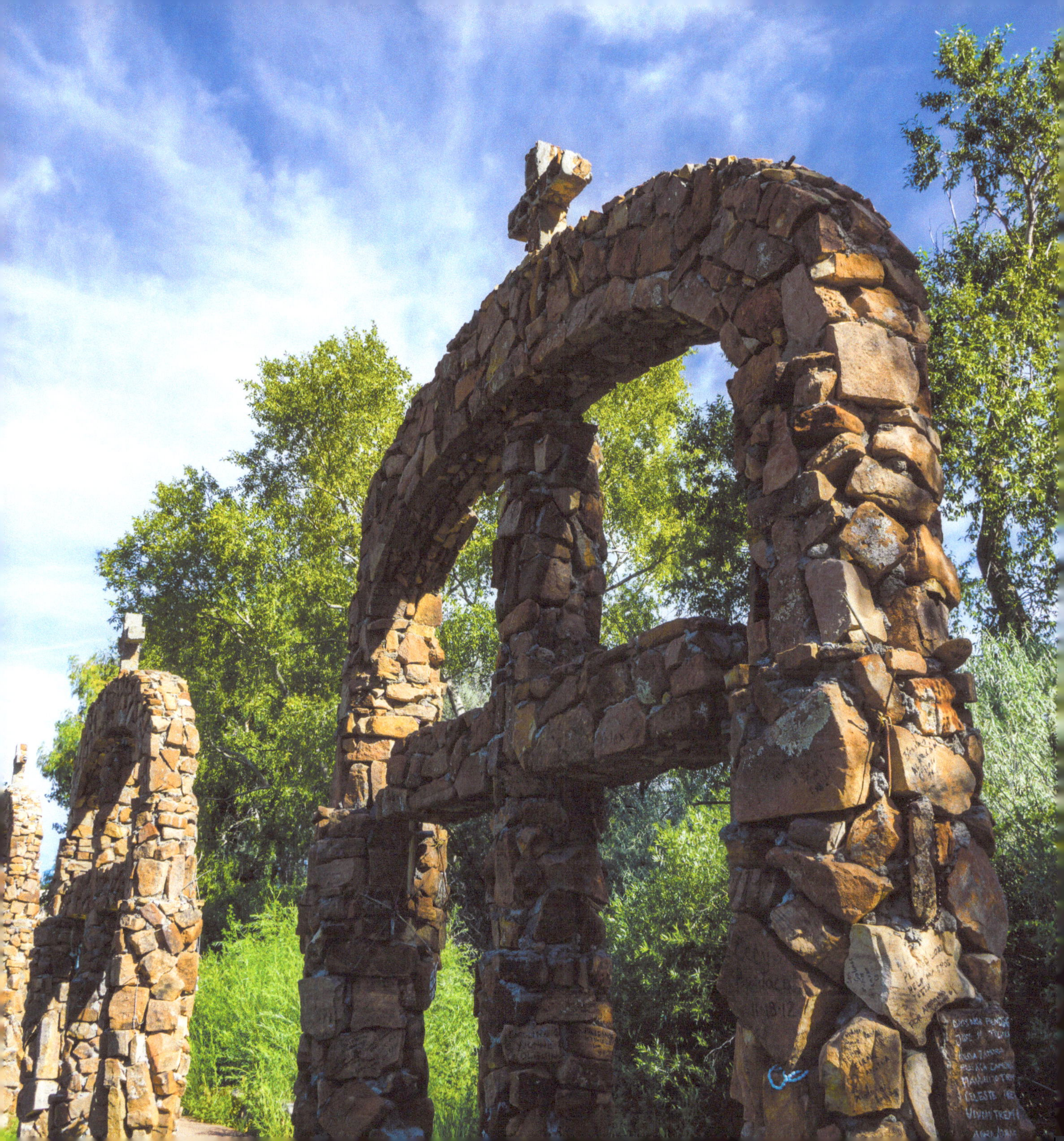

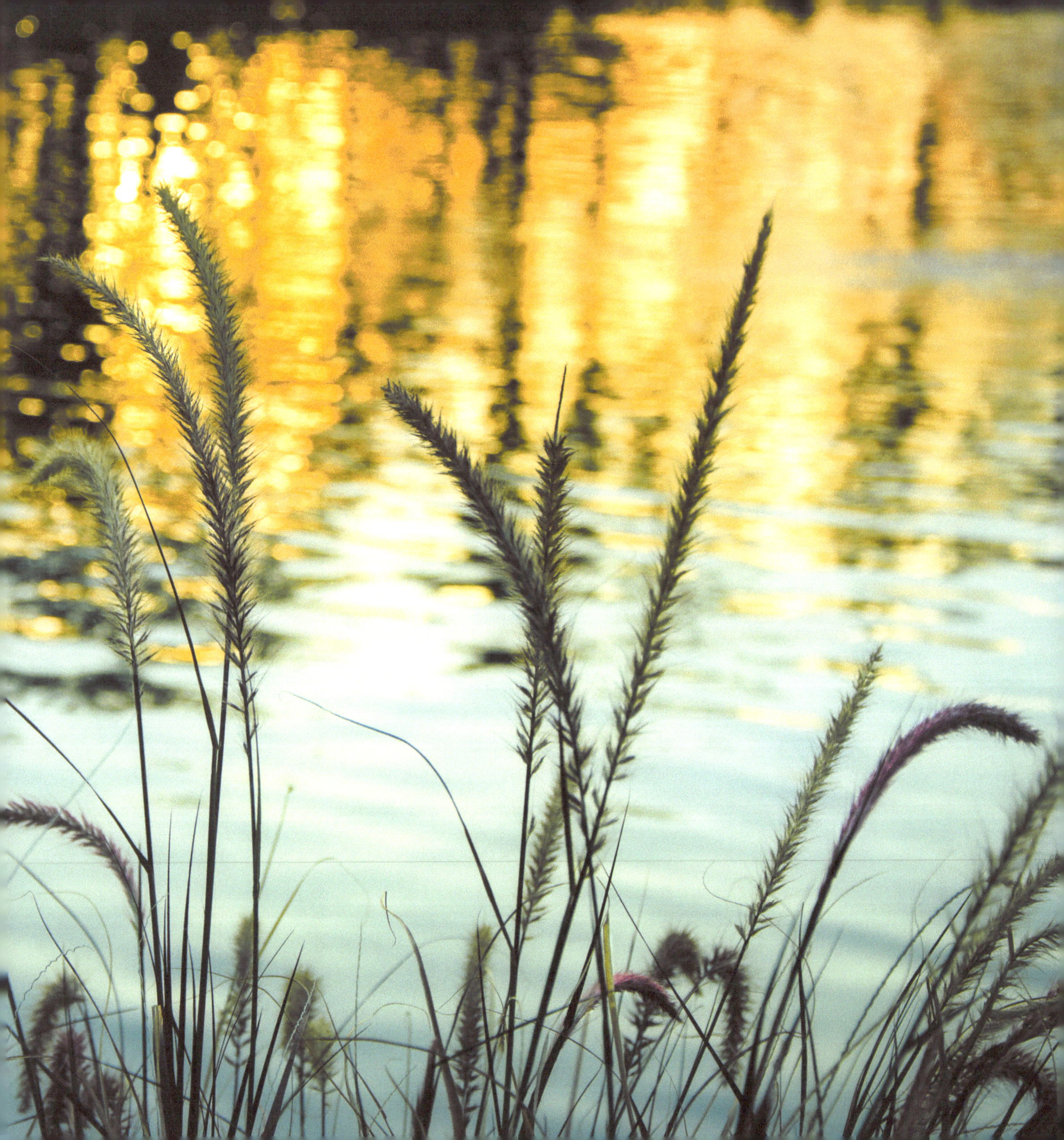

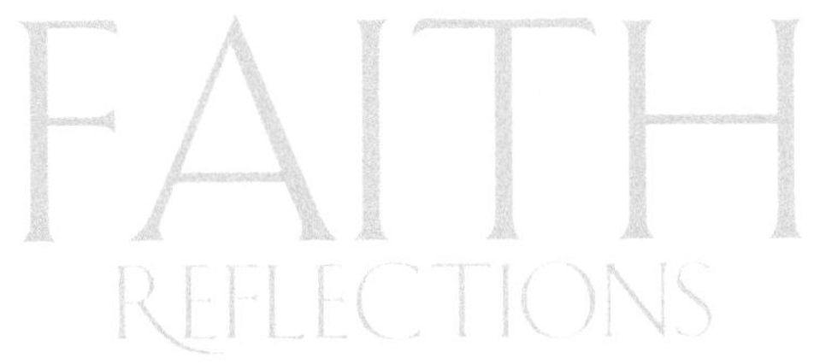

You Live By Faith

For in it the righteousness of God is revealed from faith to faith;
as it is written, "but the righteous man shall live by faith."
Romans 1:17

Have you discovered the secret of faith? It's not about how much faith you have, but where you place your faith. Ours is an objective faith in the Lord and His Word. Faith is not a feeling. A radio talk show host once said that his problem was that he had no faith. In fact, that was not his problem at all. He had plenty of faith. He just placed his faith in the wrong things. How can we experience salvation, forgiveness of sins, and eternal life? By grace through faith (Ephesians 2:8). We have the promises of God in Christ. We put our faith in Him and receive all He promises related to who He is, what He has done, and all that He says.

Lord, thank You for showing me that faith is how I live.
Today I choose to place my faith in Your promises and
not in feelings or the things of this world. In Jesus' name, Amen.

For by grace you have been saved through faith; and that not of yourselves,
it is the gift of God; not as a result of works, so that no one may boast.

Ephesians 2:8-9

Faith is the telegraphic wire which links earth to Heaven, on which God's messages of love fly so fast that before we call He answers, and while we are yet speaking He hears us.

Charles Haddon Spurgeon

Your salvation comes, not because your faith saves you, but because it links you to the Savior who saves…Let your faith, then, "throw its arms around all God has told you."

Hannah Whitall Smith — The Christian's Secret Of A Happy Life

For we walk by faith, not by sight.

2 Corinthians 5:7

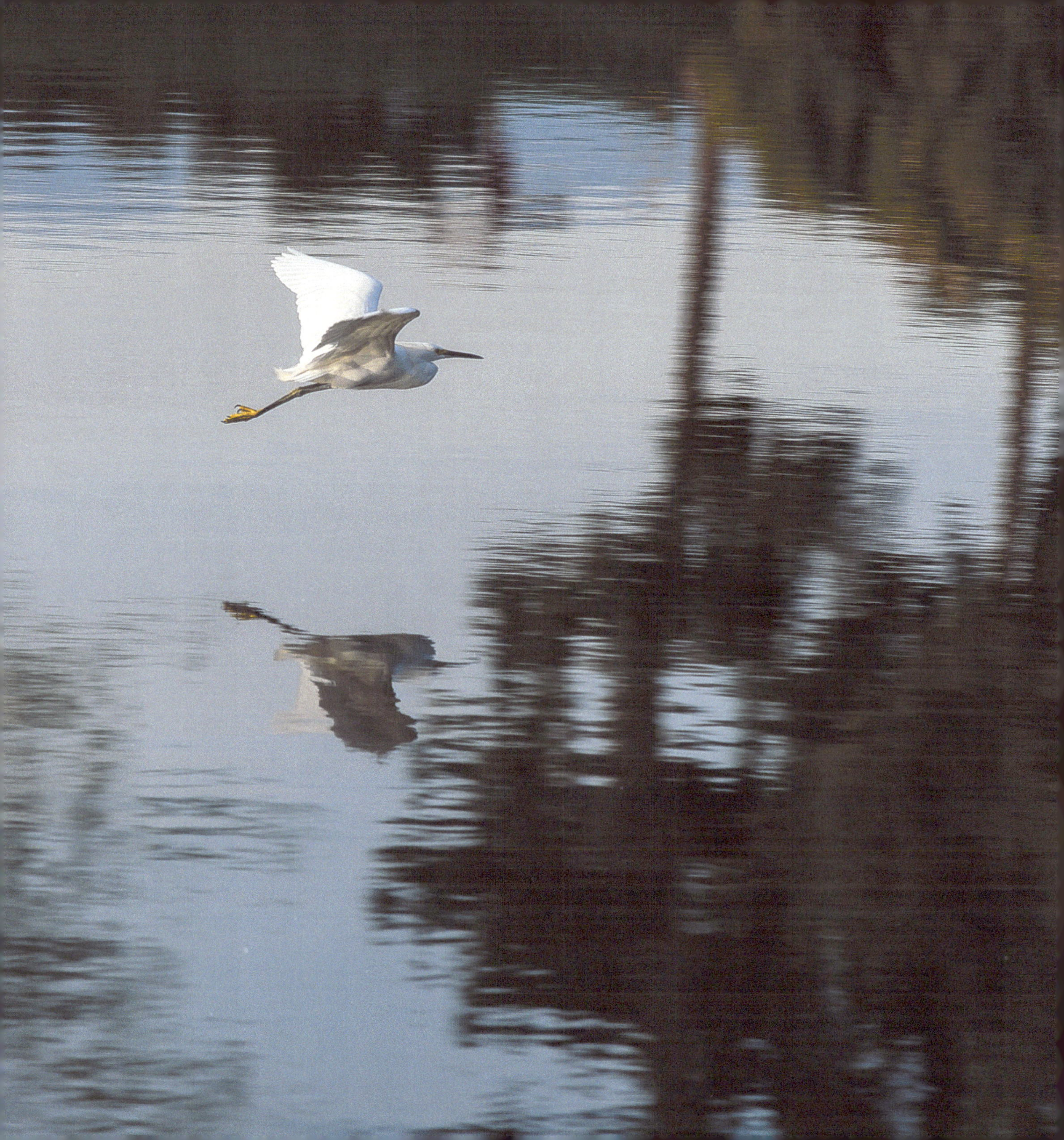

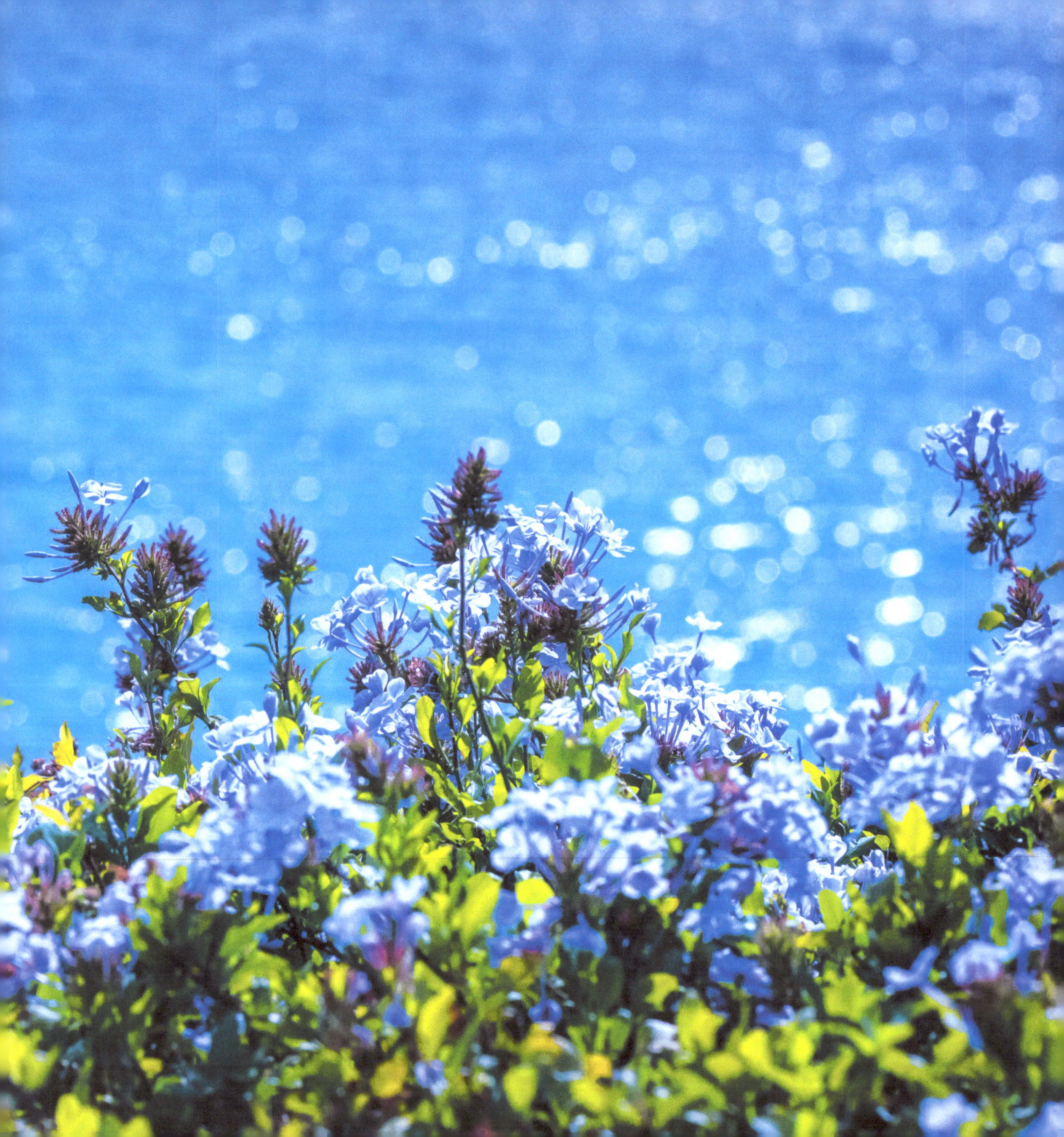

RIGHTEOUSNESS

REFLECTIONS

You Receive God's Righteousness

For in it the righteousness of God is revealed…
Romans 1:17

Have you discovered your need for God's righteousness? The world often thinks, *I'm good enough. I am righteous enough. I'm better than this person or that person.* We learn in Romans that "all have sinned and fall short of the glory of God" (Romans 3:23). There is a righteousness—the righteousness of God—that is a gift because of the finished work of Jesus Christ on the cross. The righteousness of God is His saving activity where He puts people in right standing with Himself. It is the rightness of God and rightness with God. There is only one way to receive God's righteousness—by faith.

Lord, thank You for the gift of Your righteousness, given to me by faith. Thank You for making it possible to be made right with You and doing for me what I can never do for myself. In Jesus' name, Amen.

Keep your eye steadily fixed on the infinite grandeur of Christ's finished work and righteousness. Look to Jesus and believe, look to Jesus and live! Nay, more; as you look to him, hoist your sails and buffet manfully the sea of life. Do not remain in the haven of distrust, or sleeping on your shadows in inactive repose, or suffering your frames and feelings to pitch and toss on one another like vessels idly moored in a harbor. The religious life is not a brooding over emotions, grazing the keel of faith in the shallows, or dragging the anchor of hope through the oozy tide mud as if afraid of encountering the healthy breeze. Away! With your canvas spread to the gale, trusting in Him, who rules the raging of the waters.

J.R. MacDuff

We need God's righteousness because we don't have any on our own and there is no way for us to get it on our own (Romans 3:10-12). There is, in fact, an uncrossable chasm between man and God because of sin. Because we fall short of the glory of God, on our own we cannot achieve God's righteous and holy requirement. There is such good news in Romans 3 because "Now apart from the Law the righteousness of God has been manifested, being witnessed by the Law and the Prophets, even the righteousness of God through faith in Jesus Christ for all those who believe" (Romans 3:21-22). Christ, who is your righteousness, bridged the great uncrossable chasm between our righteous and holy God and sinful man by dying on the cross.

The Proof of God's Amazing Love — Catherine Martin

I no longer count on my own righteousness through obeying the law; rather, I become righteous through faith in Christ. For God's way of making us right with himself depends on faith.

Philippians 3:9 NLT

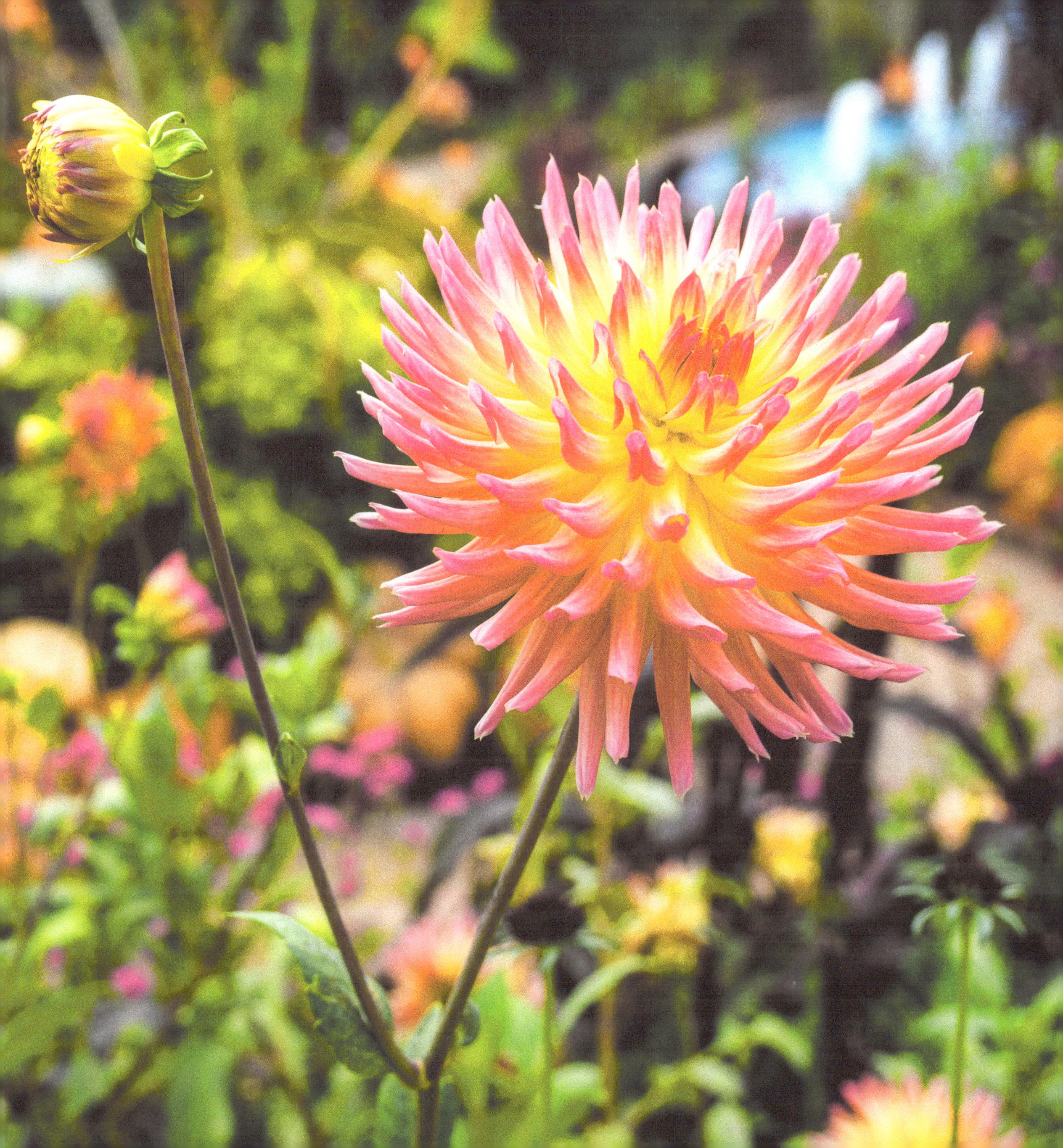

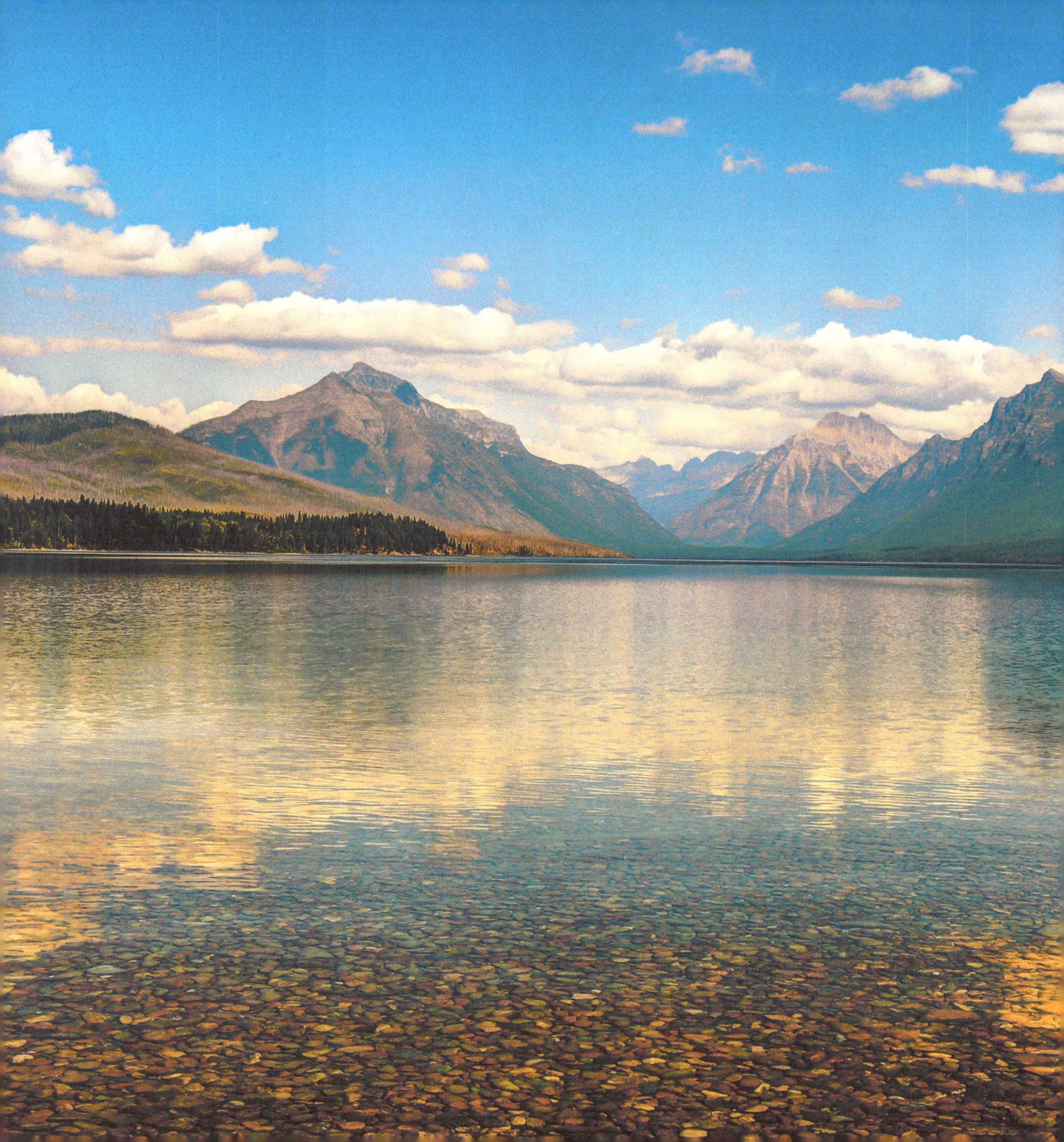

JUSTIFICATION

REFLECTIONS

You Are Justified

So then as through one transgression there resulted condemnation to all men, even so through one act of righteousness there resulted justification of life to all men.

Romans 5:18

One aspect of the good news of the gospel is that you are the recipient of God's justification. To be justified means you are acquitted, declared righteous and put in the right by God Himself. God knew you intimately beforehand and fixed His love on you. Then, God predestined or appointed you in advance to be in the likeness of His Son. He has effectually called you, justified you, and glorified you. The work is finished and nothing can rob you of it. Oh beloved, swim in the assurance and eternal security God is revealing to you today. God knows you by name and loves you.

Lord, thank You for justifying me and declaring me righteous in Your Presence.
Thank You for fixing your love on me and making me safe and secure for all eternity.
I love You and I am thrilled to be Yours both now and forevermore. In Jesus' name, Amen.

Praise to the Lord, the Almighty, the King of creation!
O my soul, praise him, for he is your health and salvation!
Come, all who hear; now to his temple draw near,
join me in glad adoration.

Praise to the Lord, above all things so wondrously reigning;
sheltering you under his wings, and so gently sustaining!
Have you not seen all that is needful has been
sent by his gracious ordaining?

Praise to the Lord, who will prosper your work and defend you;
surely his goodness and mercy shall daily attend you.
Ponder anew what the Almighty can do,
if with his love he befriends you.

Praise to the Lord! O let all that is in me adore him!
All that has life and breath, come now with praises before him.
Let the Amen sound from his people again;
gladly forever adore him.

Joachim Neander

These whom He predestined, He also called; and these whom He called, He also justified; and these whom He justified, He also glorified.

Romans 8:30

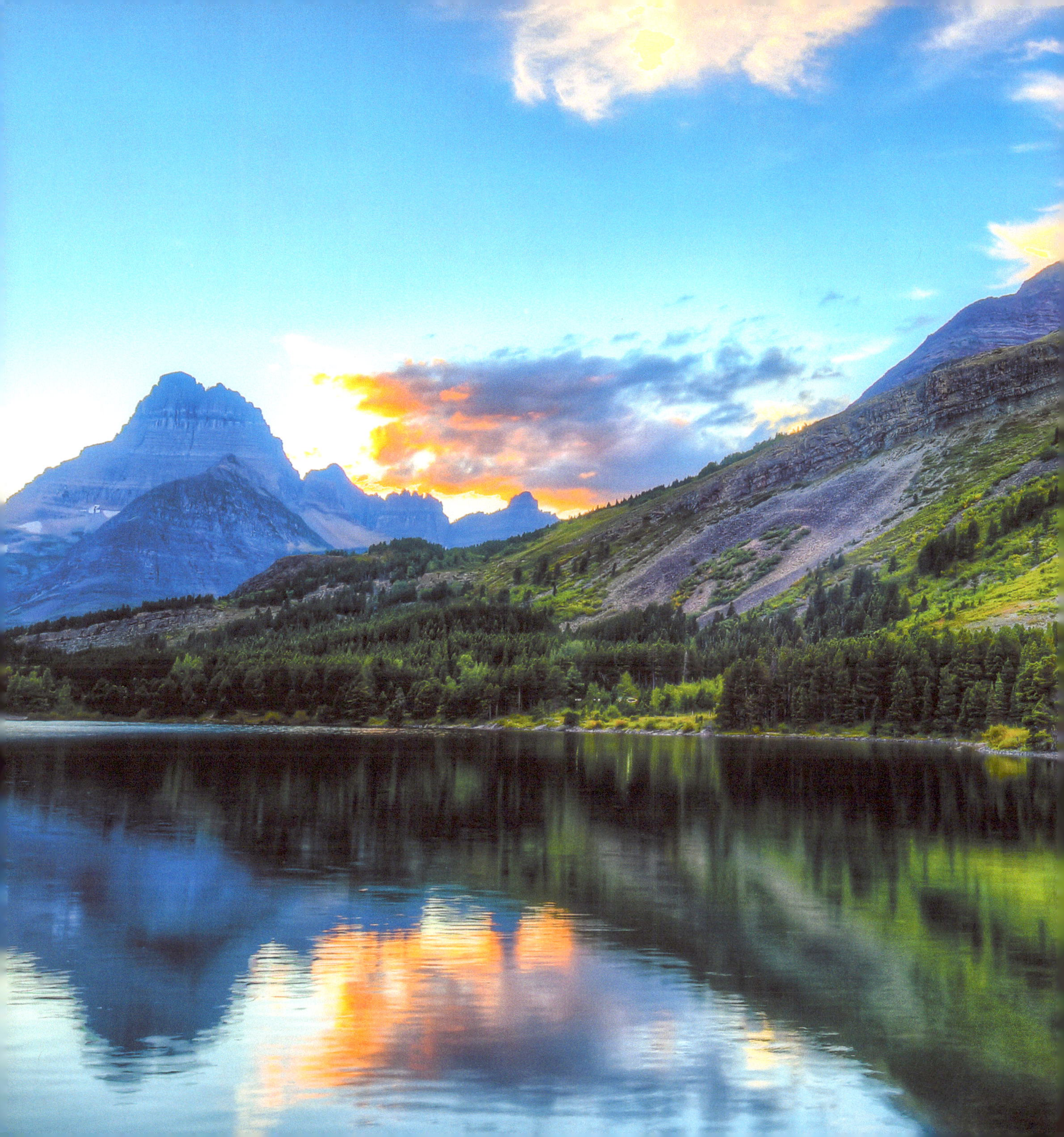

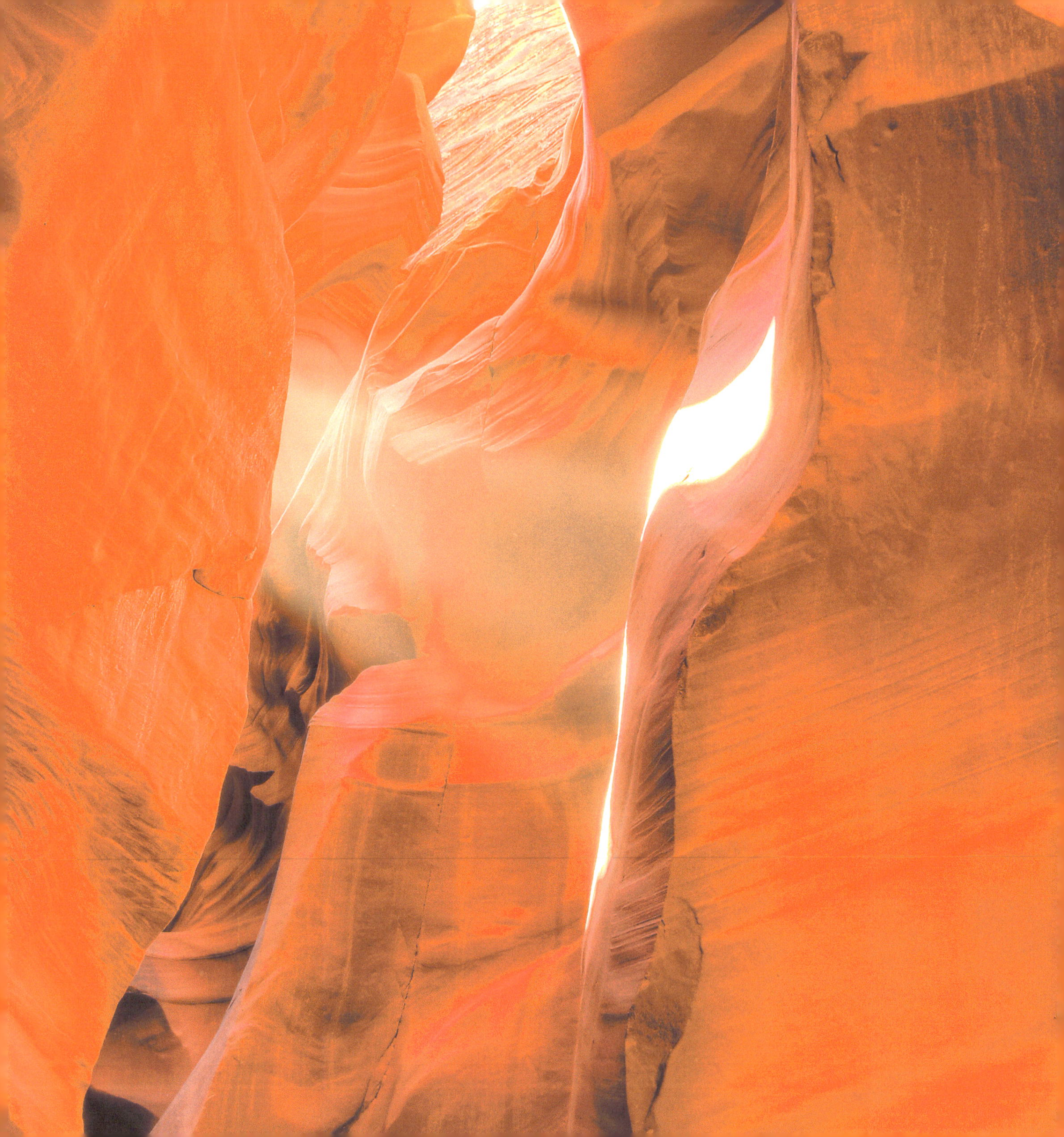

PROPITIATION
REFLECTIONS

You Have Propitiation For Your Sins

God presented Him as a propitiation through faith in His blood, to demonstrate His righteousness, because in His restraint God passed over the sins previously committed.
Romans 3:25 HCSB

How can our sins be forgiven? Jesus is our propitiation or sacrifice of atonement. When you think of "propitiation" think of the word "satisfaction." The righteous demands of a holy God are fully satisfied by Christ. Because Christ died for our sins, God's justice is satisfied and His wrath is placated and turned away. Our sins may be forgiven, we are reconciled to God, and now we are given access and communion with God. Sins can be passed over because Christ has made the atoning sacrifice and paid the penalty for sin. Rejoice in this good news of the gospel that Jesus did for you what you could never do for yourself.

Lord, thank You for dying on the cross for my sins, for being the propitiation, the sacrifice of atonement for me. You have done it all, literally accomplishing everything necessary that I may be saved. I rejoice today in my eternal relationship with You. In Jesus' Name, Amen.

And can it be that I should gain an int'rest in the Savior's blood?
Died He for me, who caused His pain? For me, who Him to death pursued?
Amazing love! How can it be that Thou, my God, should die for me?
Refrain: Amazing love! How can it be that Thou, my God, should die for me!

Tis mystery all! The Immortal dies! Who can explore His strange design
In vain the firstborn seraph tries to sound the depths of love divine!
Tis mercy all! let earth adore, let angel minds inquire no more.
Refrain: Amazing love! How can it be that Thou, my God, should die for me!

He left His Father's throne above, so free, so infinite His grace;
Emptied Himself of all but love, and bled for Adam's helpless race;
Tis mercy all, immense and free; For, O my God, it found out me.
Refrain: Amazing love! How can it be that Thou, my God, should die for me!

Long my imprisoned spirit lay fast bound in sin and nature's night;
Thine eye diffused a quick'ning ray, I woke, the dungeon flamed with light;
My chains fell off, my heart was free; I rose, went forth and followed Thee.
Refrain: Amazing love! How can it be that Thou, my God, should die for me!

No condemnation now I dread; Jesus, and all in Him is mine!
Alive in Him, my living Head, and clothed in righteousness divine,
Bold I approach the eternal throne, and claim the crown, through Christ my own.
Refrain: Amazing love! How can it be that Thou, my God, should die for me!

Charles Wesley, 1738

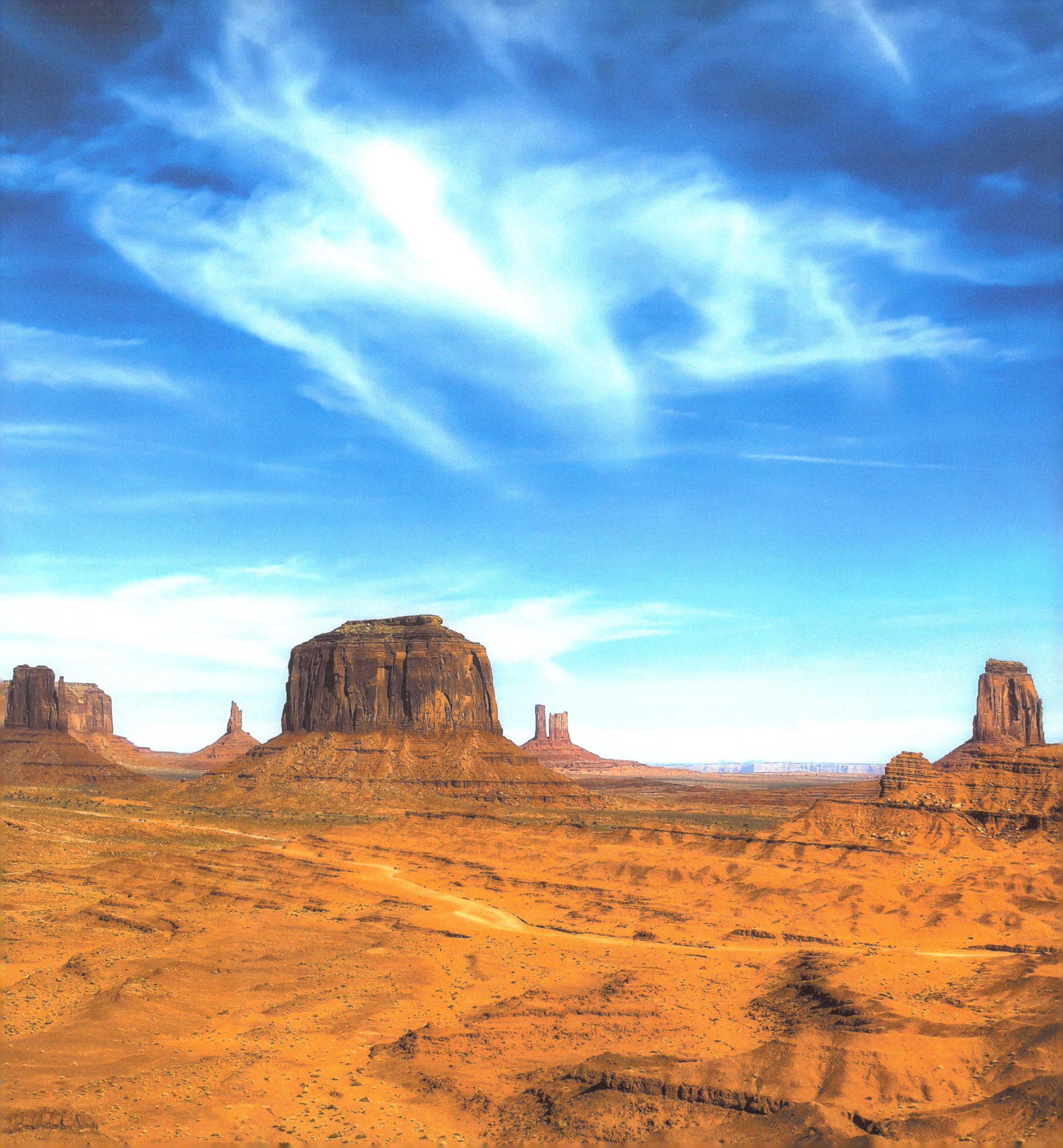

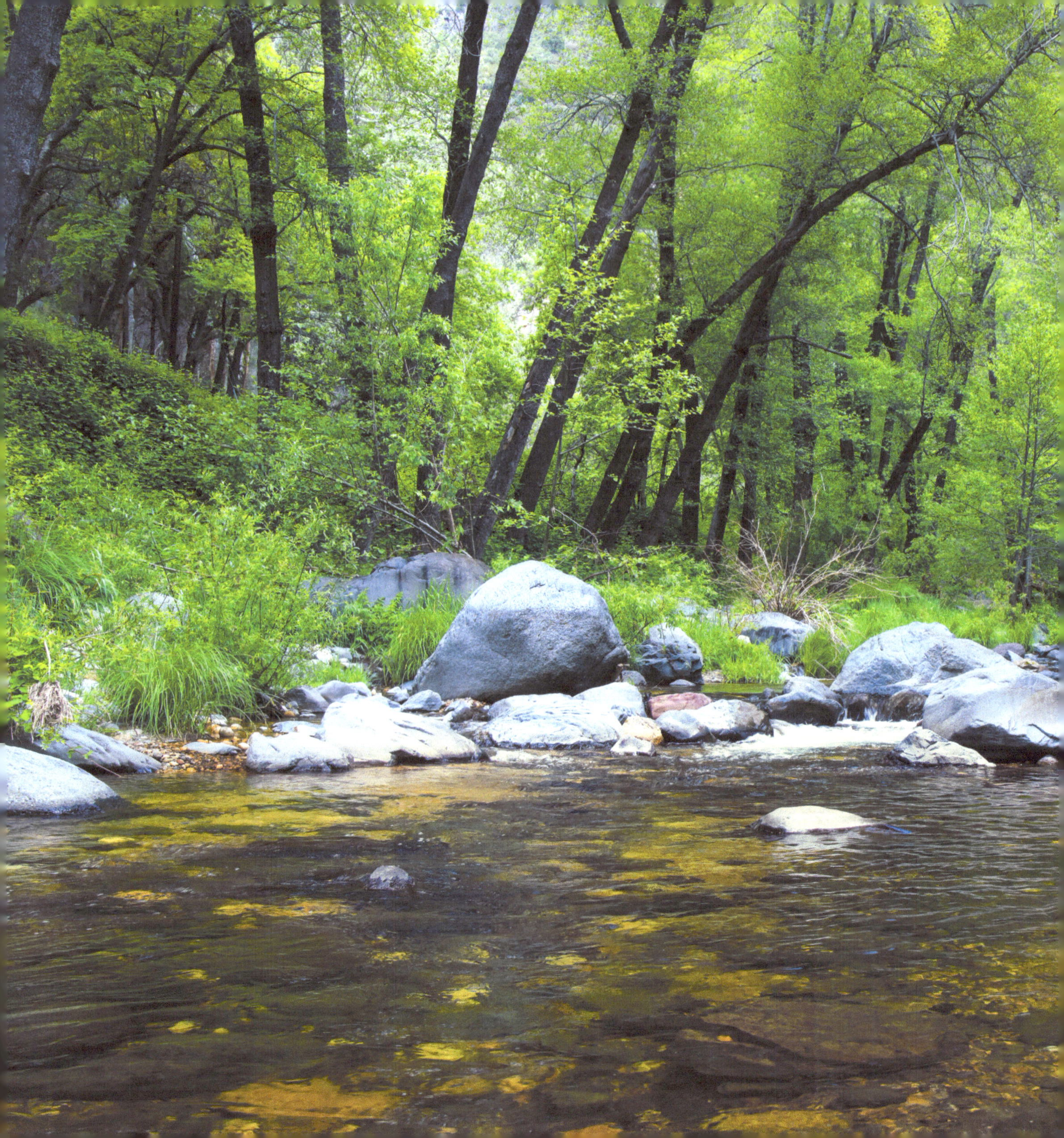

REDEMPTION

REFLECTIONS

YOU ARE REDEEMED

They are justified freely by his grace
through the redemption that is in Christ Jesus.
ROMANS 3:24 CSB

Jesus paid a debt He did not owe, and we owed a debt we could not pay. What was the price to be set free from our sin? The blood of Jesus Christ. He has accomplished redemption, having purchased believers out of the slave market of sin and setting them free. According to Hebrews 9:12 "through His own blood, He entered the holy place once for all, having obtained eternal redemption." Oh, there is such power in this good news because once you have trusted Christ as your Savior, you are redeemed and set free forever, not just for a day. Your redemption is not temporary, but eternal.

Lord, thank You for redeeming me, for purchasing me from the slave market of sin. I rejoice in being set free forever. And now, I pour out my heart of love to You and desire to know and serve You today, tomorrow, and forever. In Jesus' Name, Amen.

In Him we have redemption through His blood, the forgiveness of our trespasses, according to the riches of His grace which He lavished on us.

Ephesians 1:7-8

He erased the certificate of debt, with its obligations, that was against us and opposed to us, and has taken it away by nailing it to the cross.

Colossians 2:14 csb

Redemption means release as the result of the payment of a price. This is an essential part of the meaning of the word and it must never be omitted. The truth about us all is that we are not able to pay the adequate price, but, thank God, Another has come and paid the price for us. Here we have the great idea of substitution. The Lord Jesus Christ came to ransom us, to deliver us; He has paid the price, and so the prison in which we were held captive by the devil has been opened, and we who were slaves have been made free…All the glory must go to Christ. It is He who by His work has purchased us and set us at liberty. We are forgiven and delivered from the power of Satan by Him alone.

Romans, Exposition of Chapter 3:20-4:25, Atonement and Justification — D. Martyn Lloyd-Jones

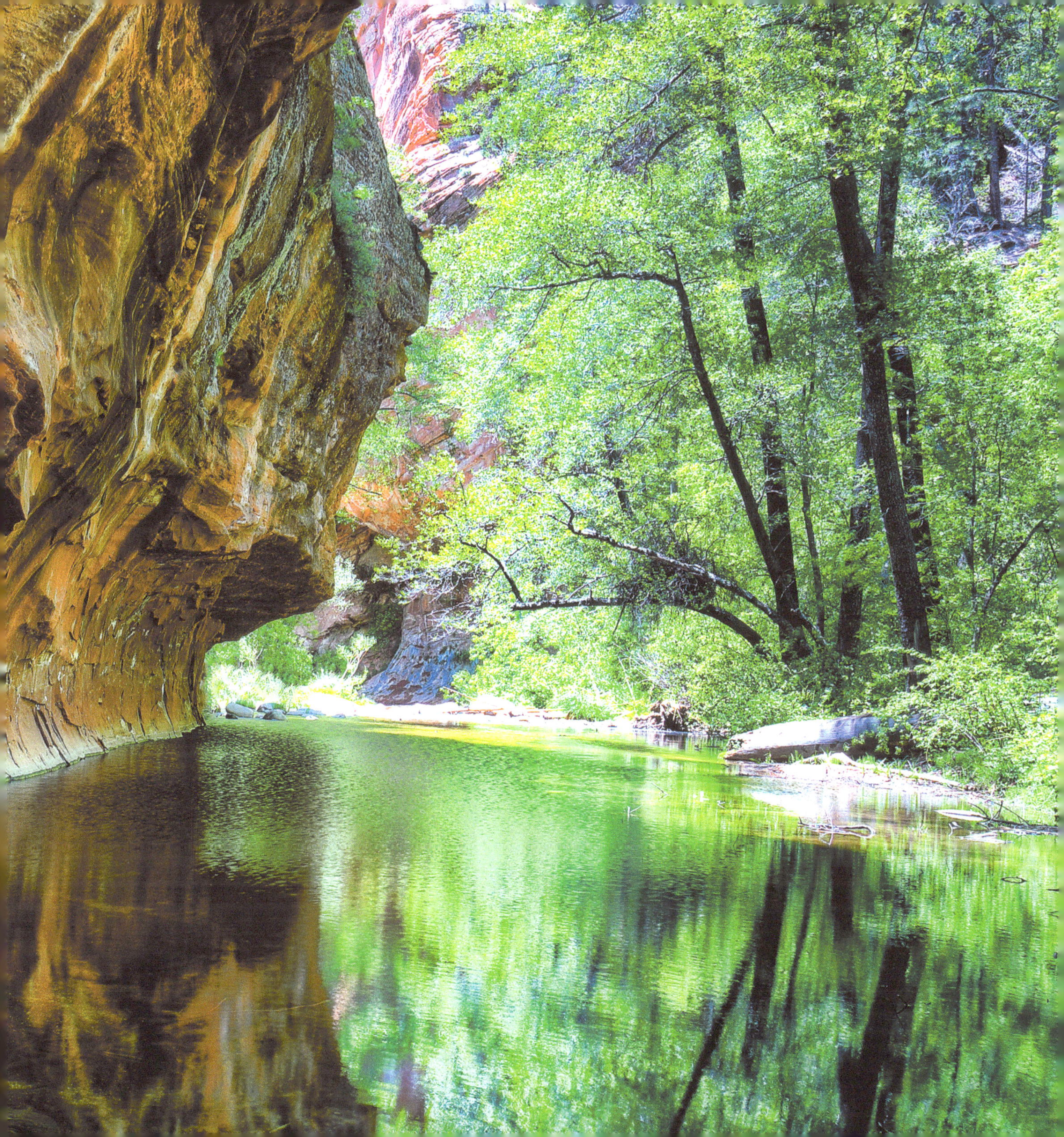

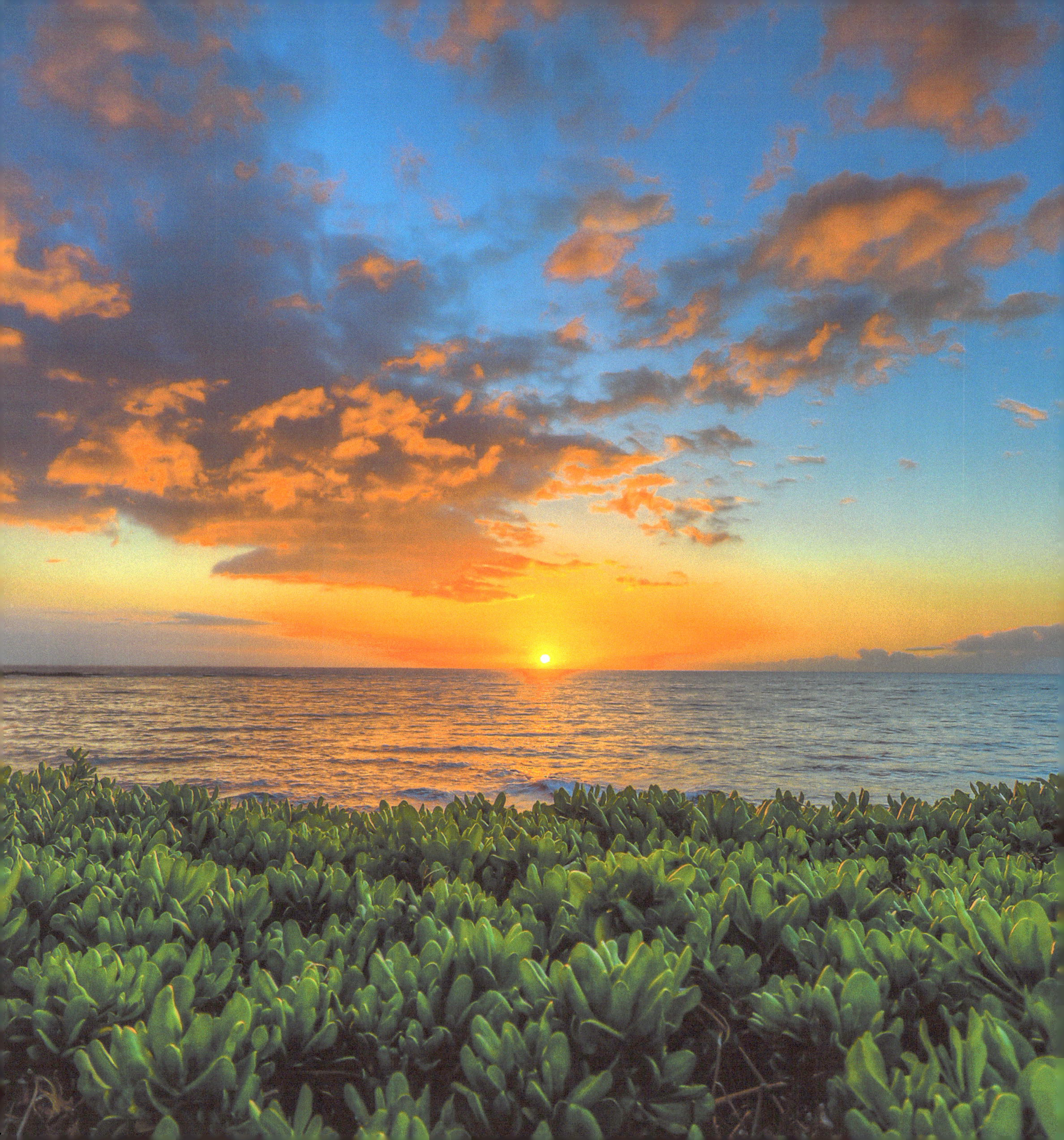

FORGIVENESS
REFLECTIONS

You Are Forgiven

Blessed and happy and to be envied are those whose iniquities are forgiven and whose sins are covered up and completely buried.
Romans 4:7 amp

One of the great truths of the gospel of Christ is that when you come to Him for salvation and trust Him as your Savior, your sins are forgiven. All mankind is guilty before a just and holy God. "All have sinned and fall short of the glory of God" (Romans 3:23). It is as though all mankind is on death row, in need of a Savior. The good news is that you have the One and Only Savior, the Lord Jesus Christ. When you confess your sins and come to Him, you are forgiven and inherit eternal life. When you realize that you are forgiven of all your sin, you are filled with gratitude to Jesus, the One who has made your newfound freedom possible.

Lord, thank You for loving me. I confess my sins to You and thank You for forgiving me and cleansing me from all unrighteousness. You have set me free and I am forever grateful to You. In Jesus' Name, Amen.

When I think of Your lavish goodness
The longings You've satisfied
The forgiveness You've granted
The promises You've kept
When I think of Your irresistible love
Your ceaseless care, Your unfailing protection...
O Lord God I want to raise flags
And fly banners and sound bugles.
I want to run with lighted torches
And praise You from the mountaintop.
I want to write symphonies and shout for joy.
I want to throw a festive party for ten thousand guests.
I want to celebrate with streamers, and bright lights
And an elaborate banquet. *Fine dear child. I'm ready.*

Precious Thoughts From The Heart — Ruth Harms Calkin

If we confess our sins, He is faithful and righteous to forgive us our sins and to cleanse us from all unrighteousness.

1 John 1:9

In Him we have redemption through His blood, the forgiveness of our trespasses, according to the riches of His grace which He lavished on us.

Ephesians 1:7-8

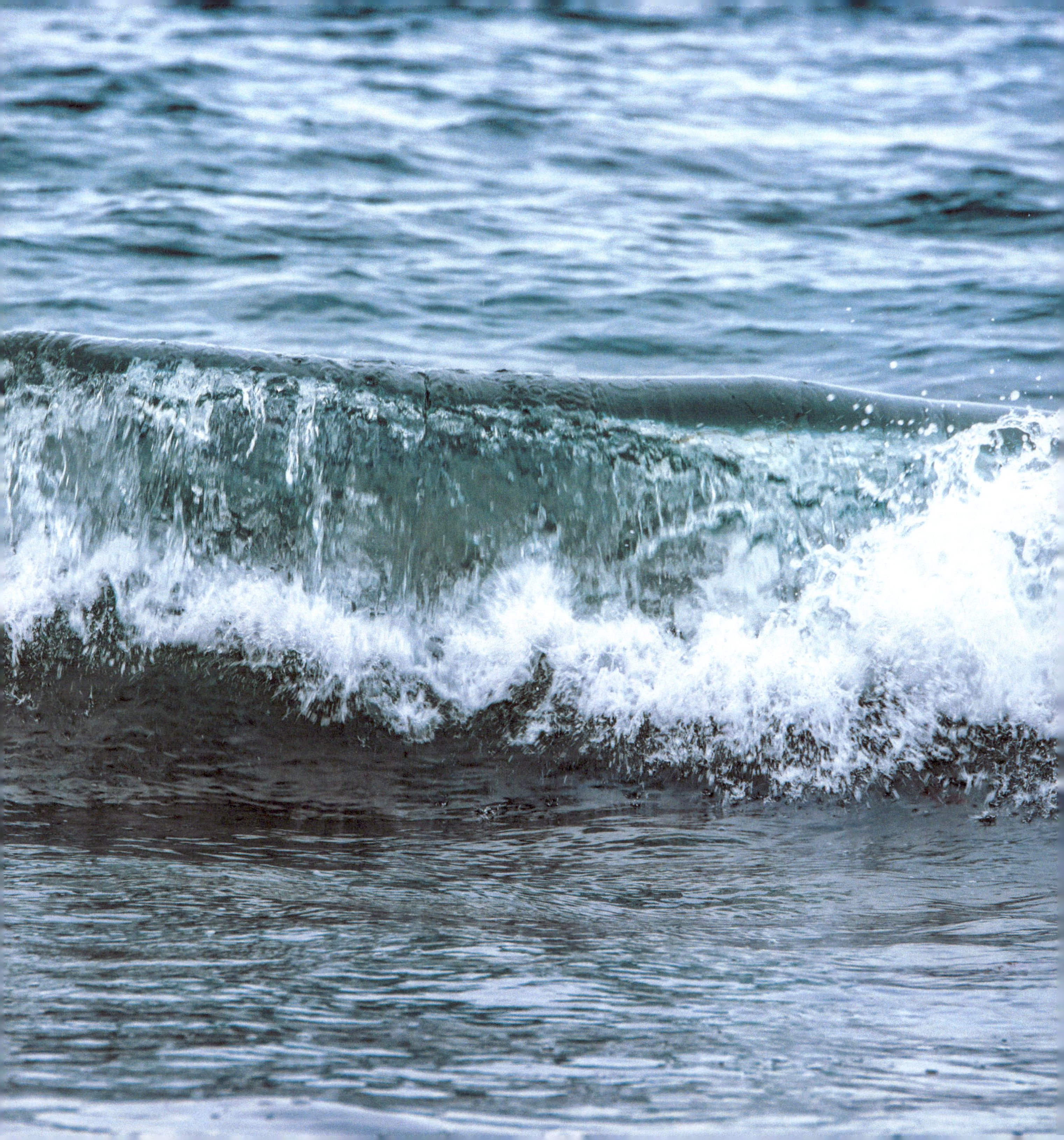

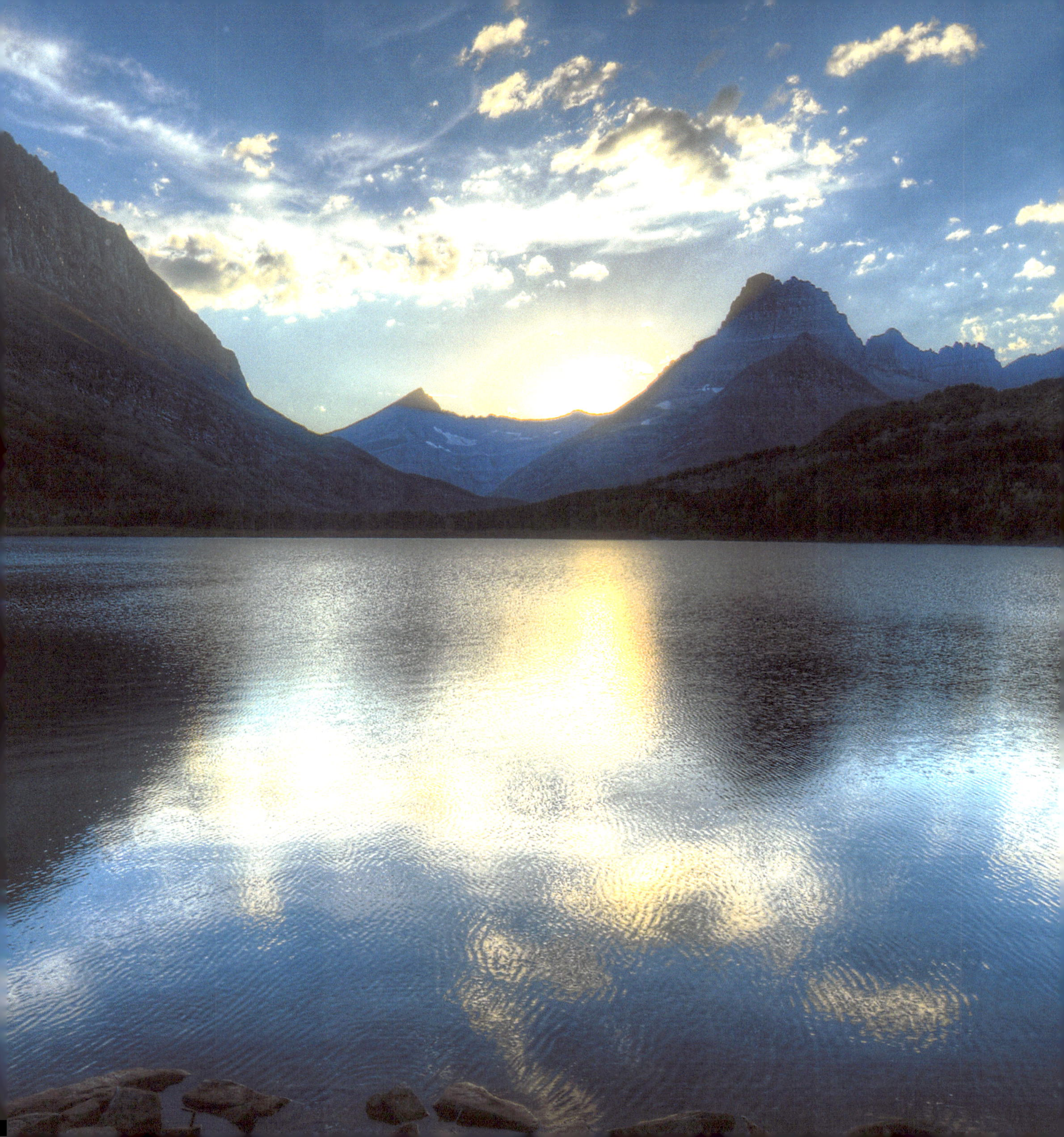

RECONCILED
REFLECTIONS

You Are Reconciled to God

For if while we were enemies we were reconciled to God through the death of His Son, more, having been reconciled, we shall be saved by His life.

Romans 5:10

Once you come to Christ and trust Him for salvation including forgiveness of sins, you receive a forever relationship with God. You experience eternal reconciliation made possible by the death of Christ on the cross for your sins. Just think about the power of the gospel as you receive this good news today. Jesus has reconciled you to God, changing the relationship from enmity to friendship, from hostility to peace and divine favor. Now you are free to enjoy your relationship with the Lord, spend quiet time with Him in His Word, and talk with Him in prayer. His daily presence in your life and His friendship are treasures to cherish forever.

Lord, I am so thankful for our relationship. I have a newfound freedom to enjoy quiet time alone with You. I love reading and studying Your Word, listening to You teach me truth, and then pouring out my heart in prayer to You. In Jesus' Name, Amen.

We may hold our heads high in the light of God's love
because of the reconciliation which Christ has made.

Romans 5:11 Phillips

Jesus gave a dramatic picture of God's amazing love and His heart for you in His parable about the prodigal son in Luke 15:11-32. In His story, Jesus described a father with two sons. The younger son demanded his inheritance, left home, and eventually lost all his money with wild living. Finally, he came to his senses and returned home, hoping to be hired as a servant. But the prodigal underestimated his father's love. It was always there, but he never saw it or realized the depth of it until now. "And while he was still a long way off, his father saw him coming. Filled with love and compassion, he ran to his son, embraced him, and kissed him" (Luke 15:20). Do you see the depth of God's love for you? His love does not hold us at arm's length, but initiates a run towards us and a reconciliation with us, embracing us with His everlasting arms, and expressing deep affection.

The Proof of God's Amazing Love — Catherine Martin

The father's actions are a drama of reconciliation that can restore the boy to his home and to his community. After this scene, no one in the village can reject or despise him.

The Cross and the Prodigal — Kenneth Bailey

If Love can die for us when "we were in a repulsive state of impotence" much more now that we are reconciled will it cherish and keep us.

Romans, A Devotional Commentary — W.H. Griffith Thomas

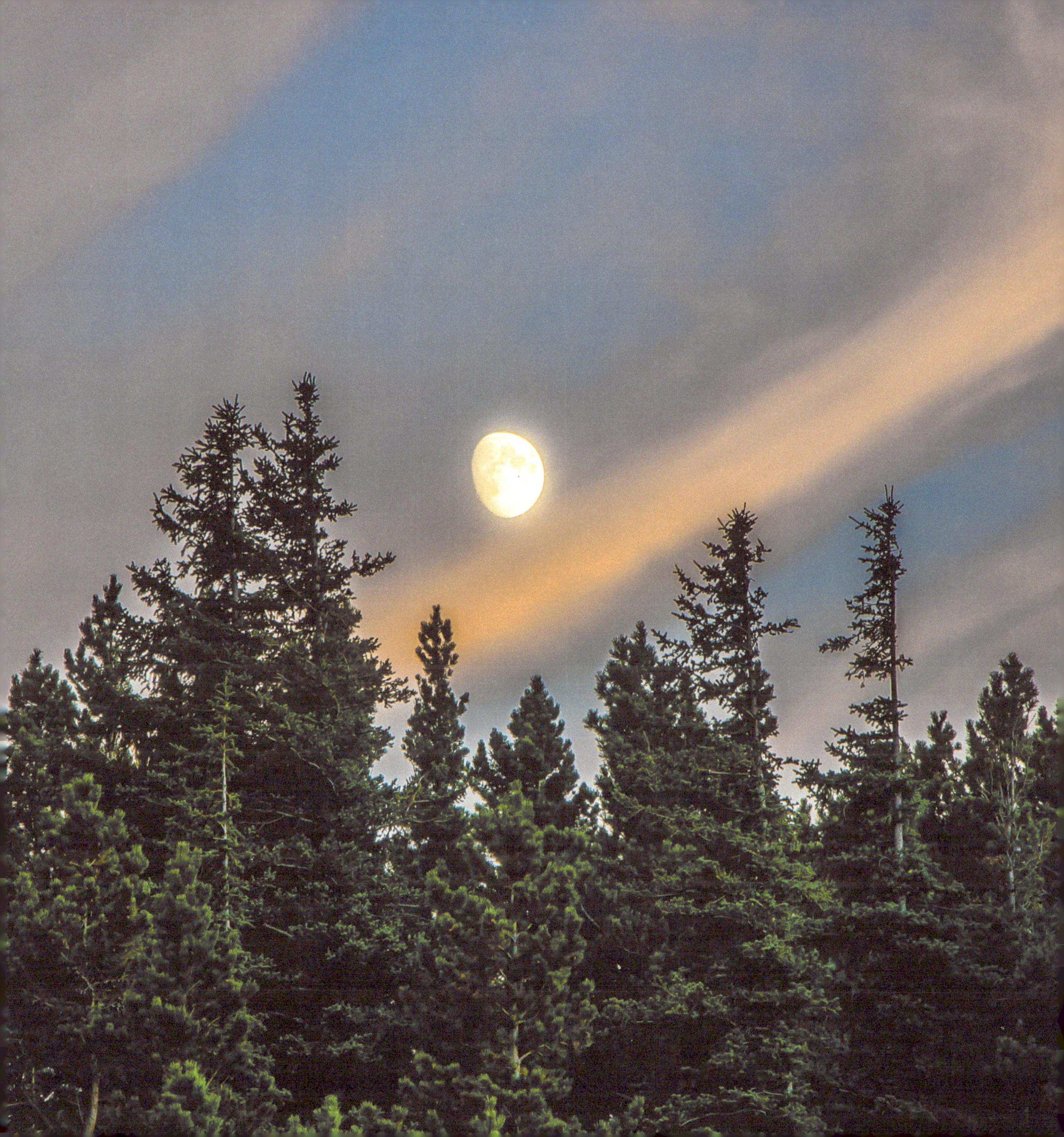

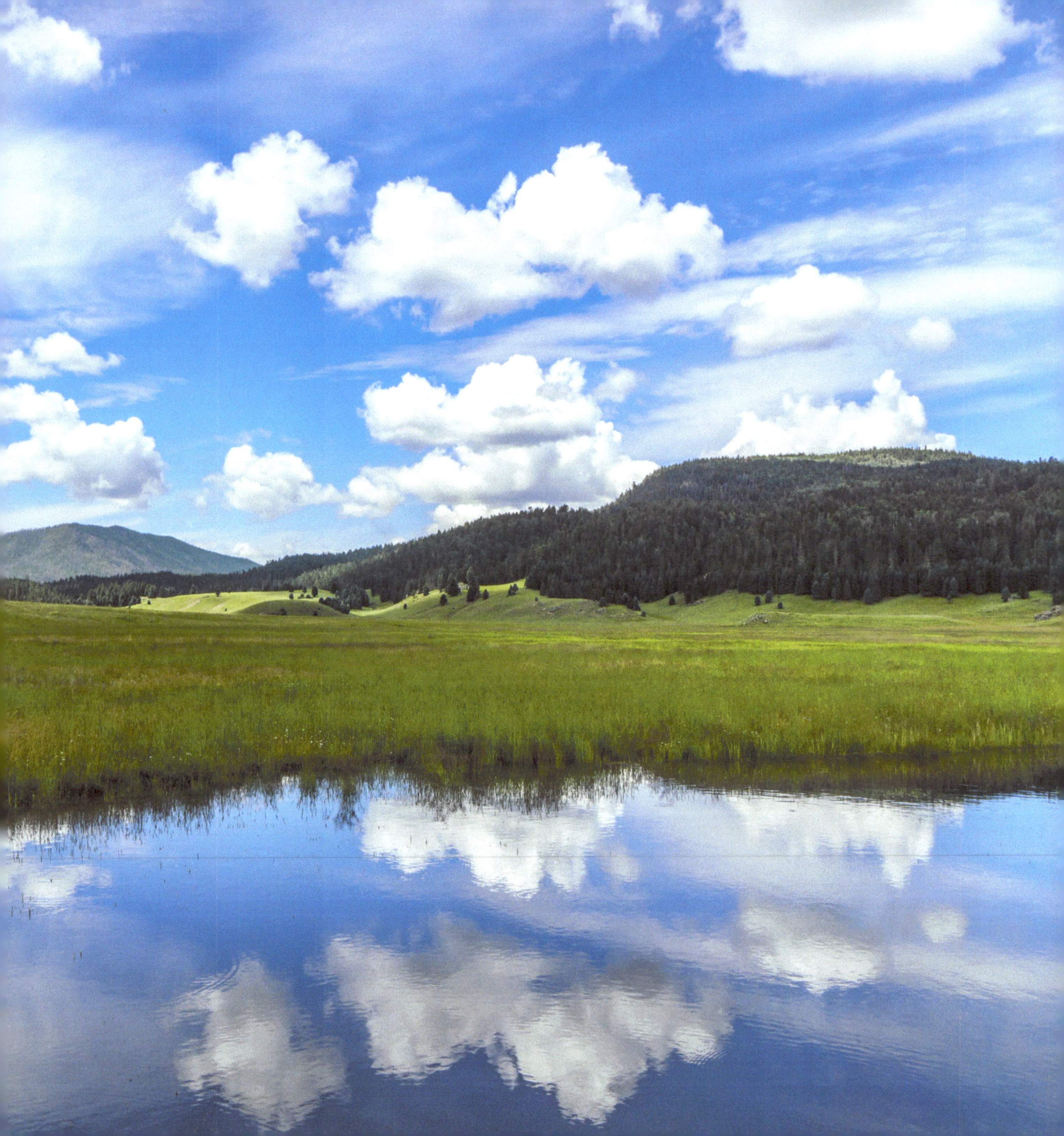

GRACE REFLECTIONS

YOU STAND IN GRACE

Through him we have also obtained access by faith into this grace in which we stand, and we rejoice in hope of the glory of God.

ROMANS 5:2

Salvation is a gift given by grace as one trusts in the finished work of Christ. You can't earn forgiveness of sins and eternal life, but you can receive these gifts by grace through faith. He offers them to you as a gift because of His amazing love for you. G-R-A-C-E has been defined as *God's Riches At Christ's Expense*. Standing in God's grace is an unshakeable position. Nothing can touch you and nothing can knock you down. You are held strong by God and God alone. The land of God's grace is a garden of beauty where you breathe in the pure air of peace, hope and the love of God. You are never without His grace, so enjoy His grace every day.

Lord, I am so thankful for the grace you have bestowed on me. I love this place of safety where my position is unshakeable and untouchable because I am held strong in You. Help me to receive all the gifts of your grace every day. In Jesus' Name, Amen.

Amazing grace, how sweet the sound, that saved a wretch like me
I once was lost but now am found, was blind, but now I see

John Newton, 1779

There is no more wonderful word than "grace." It means unmerited favour, or kindness shown to one who is utterly undeserving. Here again the purely gratuitous character of our salvation is brought out. It is something that results from the sole exercise of the spontaneous love of God. It is not merely a free gift, but a free gift to those who deserve the exact opposite, and it is given to us while we are "without hope and without God in the world."

Romans, Exposition of Chapter 3:20-4:25, Atonement and Justification — D. Martyn Lloyd-Jones

Grace is God's love in action. When you think of grace, think of God's arms open wide to you, regardless of what you have done. Grace opens the floodgates and allows God's endless love to pour into our lives, moment by moment, on into eternity. You have grace for today, grace for tomorrow, and grace forever. Now that's an extravagant, outrageous grace.

The Proof of God's Amazing Love — Catherine Martin

For by grace you have been saved through faith; and that not of yourselves, it is the gift of God.

Ephesians 2:8

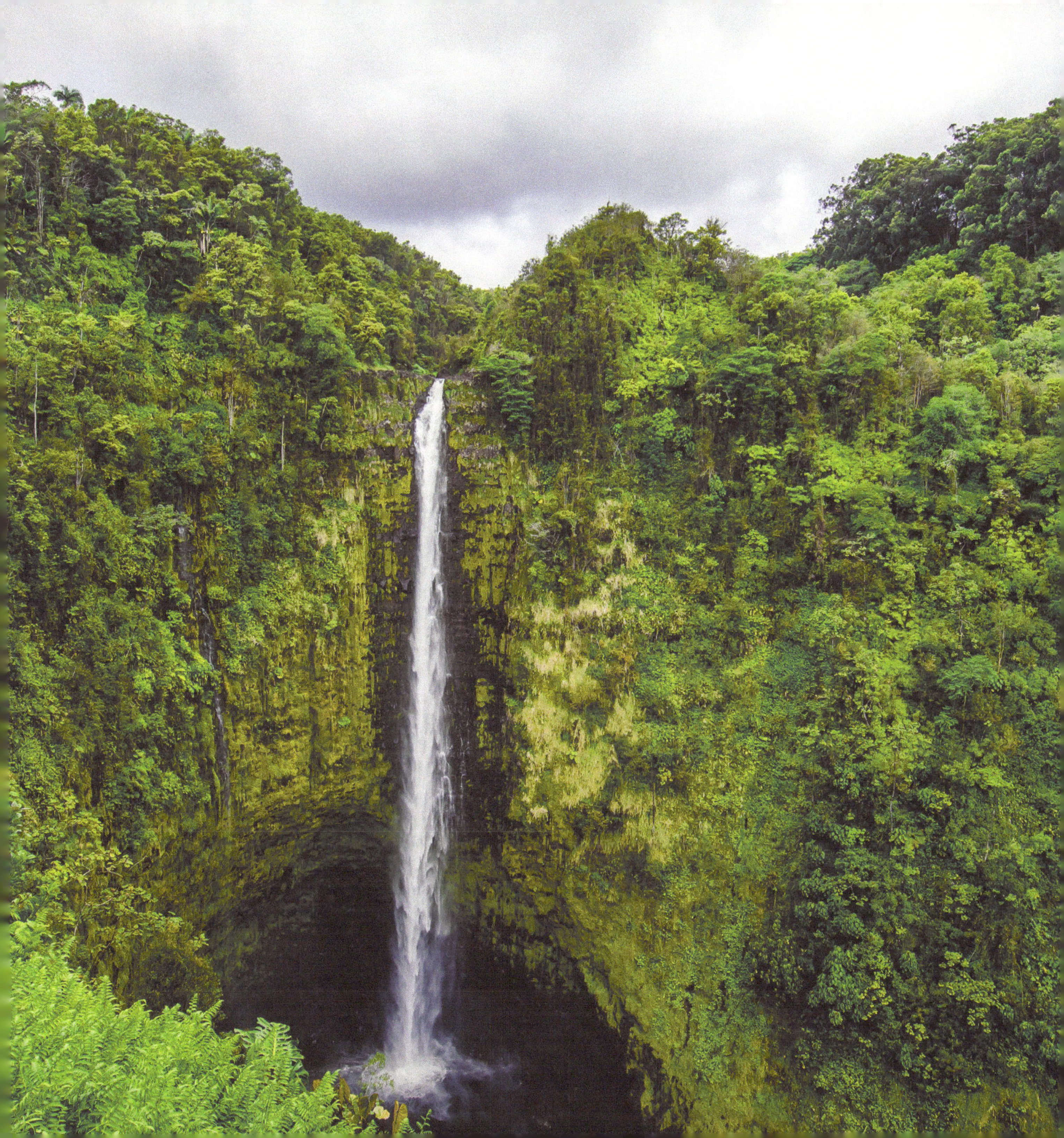

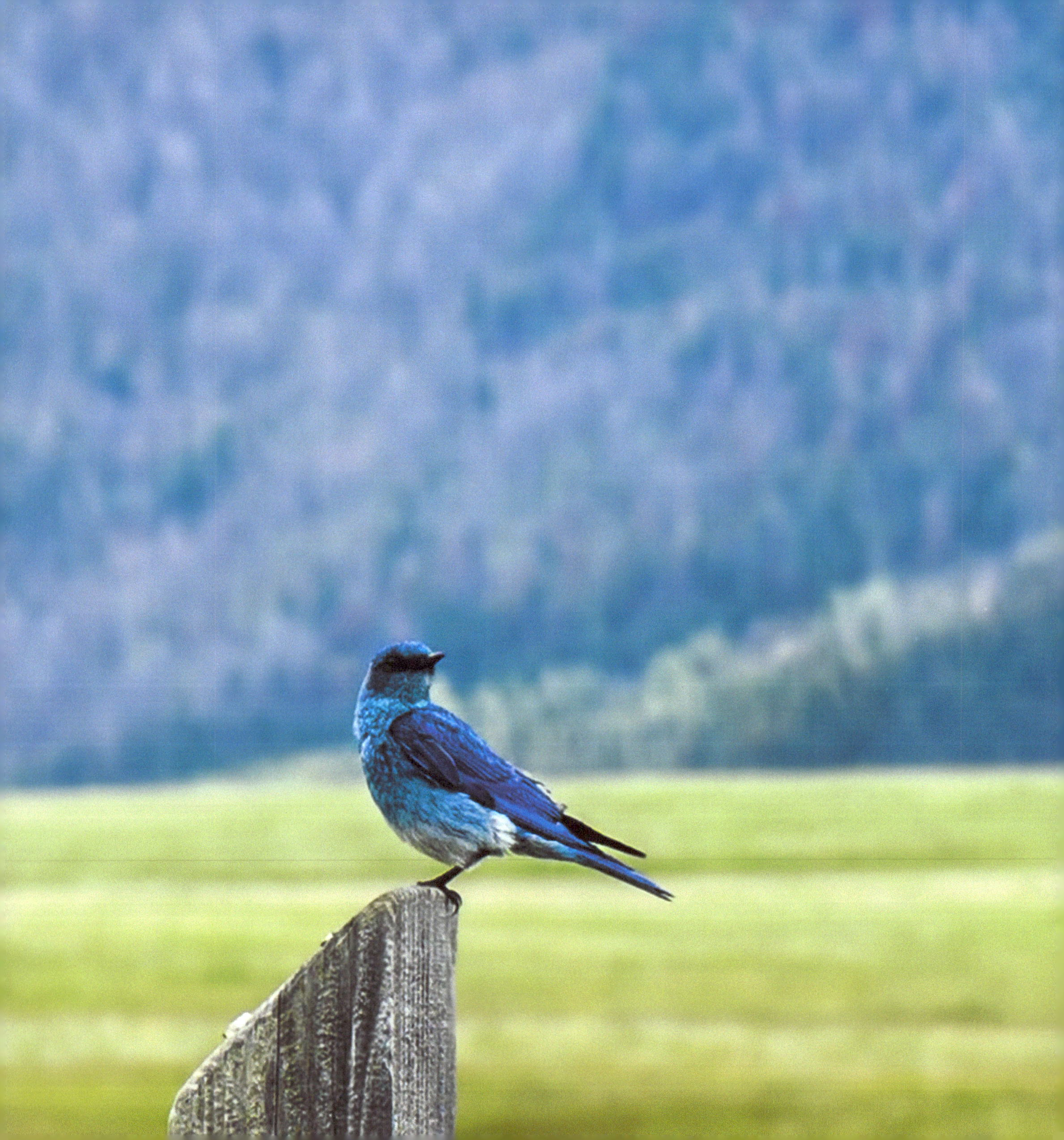

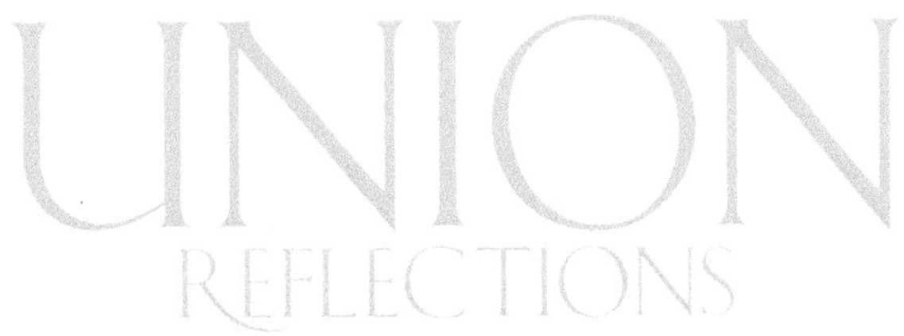

You Are United with Christ

For if we have become united with Him in the likeness of His death, certainly we shall also be in the likeness of His resurrection.
Romans 6:5

One of the most exciting truths revealed in the gospel is that once you are saved by grace through faith in Christ, you have a whole new identity. You are brought into a vital saving relationship, incorporated into Christ, and united with Him forever. Christ now lives in you through the Holy Spirit. Your union with Christ means you have been "freed from sin." You are acquitted because you died with Christ, you were raised to new life with Christ, and now you live forever with Him. William R. Newell, Moody Bible Institute, says that "to be joined in life with the Risen Christ, and thus daily, hourly, to walk is a wonder and the blessed portion of all true Christians."

Lord, I am profoundly moved to realize that I am now united with You and that moment by moment You walk and talk with me. I am never alone and You are always here with me, living in and through me. Help me be more aware of Your Presence in my life each day. In Jesus' Name, Amen.

I have been crucified with Christ; and it is no longer I who live, but Christ lives in me; and the life which I now live in the flesh I live by faith in the Son of God, who loved me and gave Himself up for me.

Galatians 2:20

When we place our trust in Jesus Christ for salvation from sin, we are said to be enveloped by Him in a spiritual sense. In a very real way, our identity becomes united with His, such that His experience becomes ours. He died and we died with Him. He rose from the dead to a new kind of life, and so shall we. By virtue of our identification with Jesus Christ, His death, and His resurrection, we have been emancipated from bondage to sin. Identity with Christ began with belief, but it has ongoing consequences.

Swindoll's New Testament Insights: Romans — Charles R. Swindoll

As you think about your new identity, united with Christ, and living in the land of grace, just imagine the intimacy that is possible with Christ. You can walk and talk with Him in the garden of grace and grow daily in your relationship with Him. Peter encourages you with these words, "But grow in the grace and knowledge of our Lord and Savior Jesus Christ" (2 Peter 3:18). As you grow, you will affirm who you are in Christ, and you will be able to say, "Because of God's grace I am secure, forgiven, accepted, and loved forever by God. I am always in God's audience, united with Christ, and indwelt by the Holy Spirit. I stand in extravagant grace, the perfect environment for spiritual growth. I am blessed with every spiritual blessing and have everything I need. I am God's beautiful masterpiece, designed for His purposes and plans. I have the hope of heaven where I will live with Christ forever. Believe it, receive it, and live it.

The Proof of God's Amazing Love — Catherine Martin

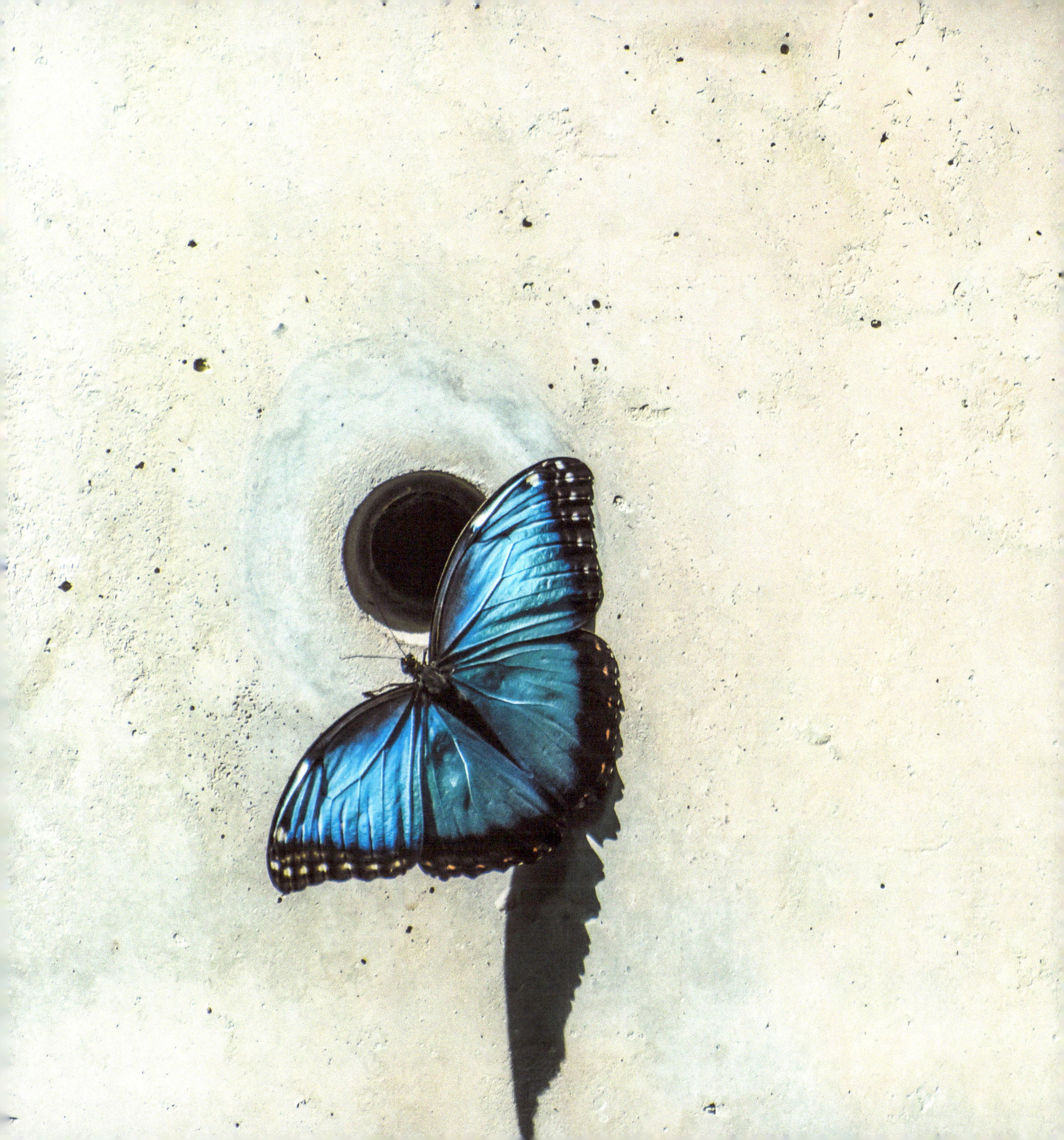

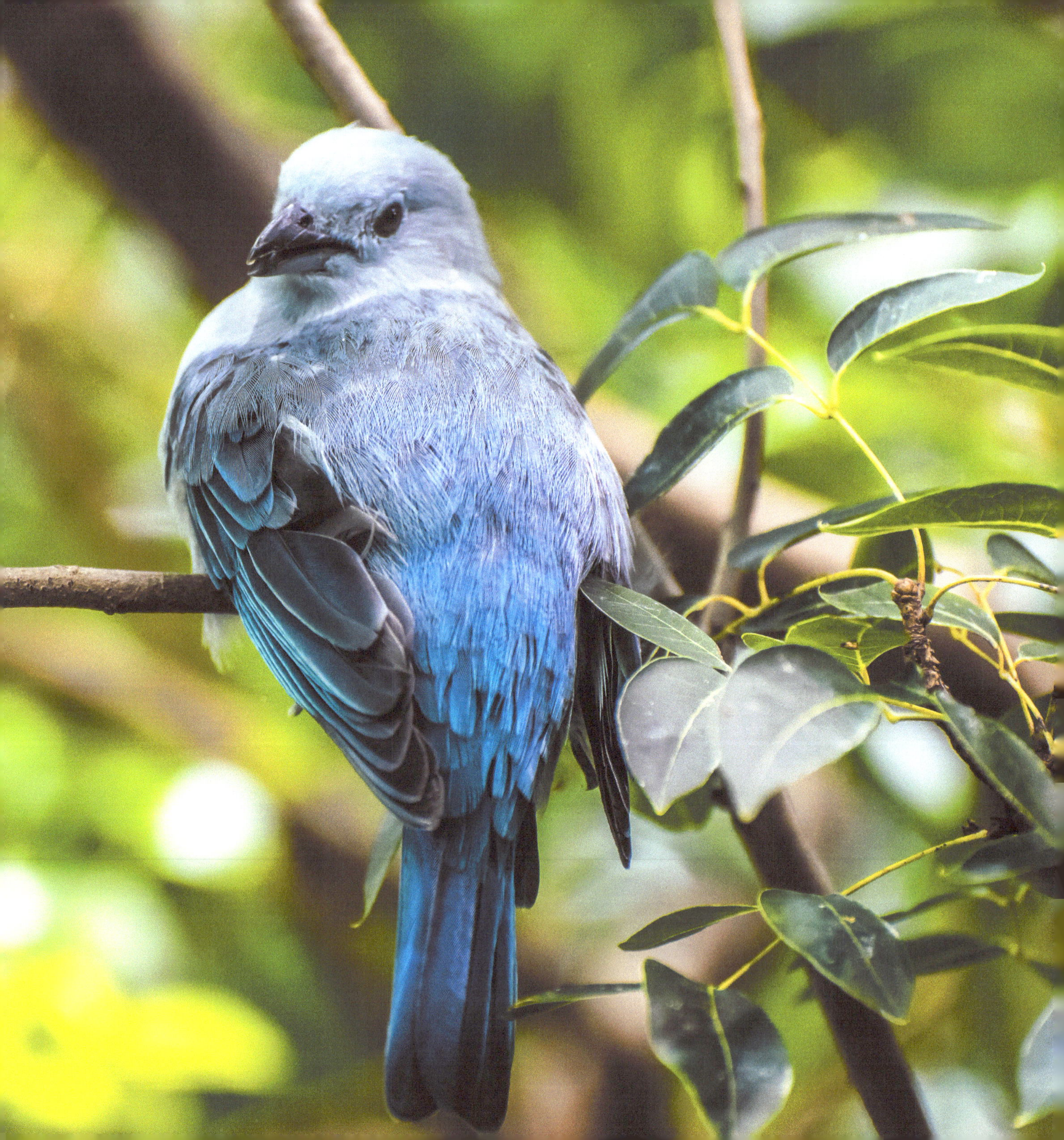

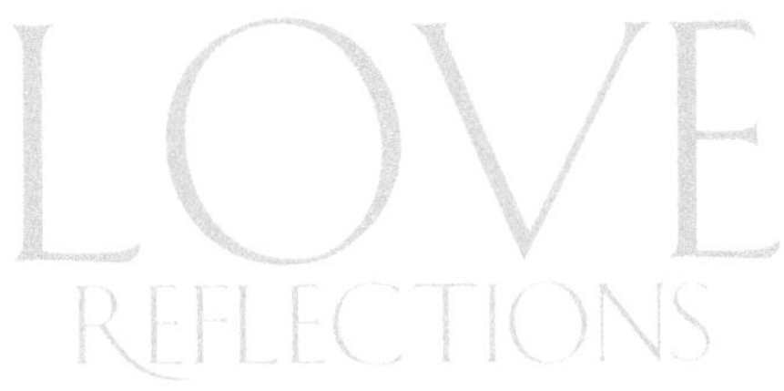

You Are Loved By God

The proof of God's amazing love is this;
that it was while we were sinners that Christ died for us.
Romans 5:8 Phillips

God's love is greater than we will ever fully understand. In fact, you might describe it as unfathomable and incomprehensible. If you ask the question, "How much does God love me?," just look at the truths of Romans 5:8 and Jesus, nailed to the cross to die for our sins, and you can answer "That much!" Jesus said it Himself when He told Nicodemus, a teacher of Israel, who was inquiring how one could be born again: "For God so loved the world, that He gave His only begotten Son, that whoever believes in Him shall not perish, but have eternal life." (John 3:16). You may hold your head high in the light of His love for you (Romans 5:11).

Lord, thank You that I can know without question that You love me. You showed me just how much by dying on the cross for me. I can never doubt Your love no matter what I am facing today. I love You with all my heart. In Jesus' Name, Amen.

Overwhelming victory is ours through Christ, who loved us. And I am convinced that nothing can ever separate us from God's love. Neither death nor life, neither angels nor demons, neither our fears for today nor our worries about tomorrow—not even the powers of hell can separate us from God's love. No power in the sky above or in the earth below—indeed, nothing in all creation will ever be able to separate us from the love of God that is revealed in Christ Jesus our Lord.

Romans 8:37-39 NLT

O Love that will not let me go, I rest my weary soul in thee.
I give thee back the life I owe, that in thine ocean depths
its flow may richer, fuller be.

George Matheson

"Like an apple tree among the trees of the forest, so is my beloved among the young men. In his shade I took great delight and sat down, and his fruit was sweet to my taste. He has brought me to his banquet hall, and his banner over me is love…When I found him whom my soul loves; I held on to him and would not let him go" (Song of Solomon 2:3-4, 3:4). The Song of Solomon is considered by some commentators to be a picture of our relationship with Christ. H.A. Ironside, in his beautiful *Addresses on the Song of Solomon*, writes that the marriage relationship is used throughout Scripture "to set forth our union and communion with the Eternal Lover of our souls." He speaks of our intimate relationship with Christ when he writes: "The more we get to know of Christ, the more we delight in His presence." He calls the banqueting house "the place of the soul's deep enjoyment when all else is shut out, and Christ's all-satisfying love fills the spirit's vision, and the entire being is taken up with Himself."

The Proof of God's Amazing Love — Catherine Martin

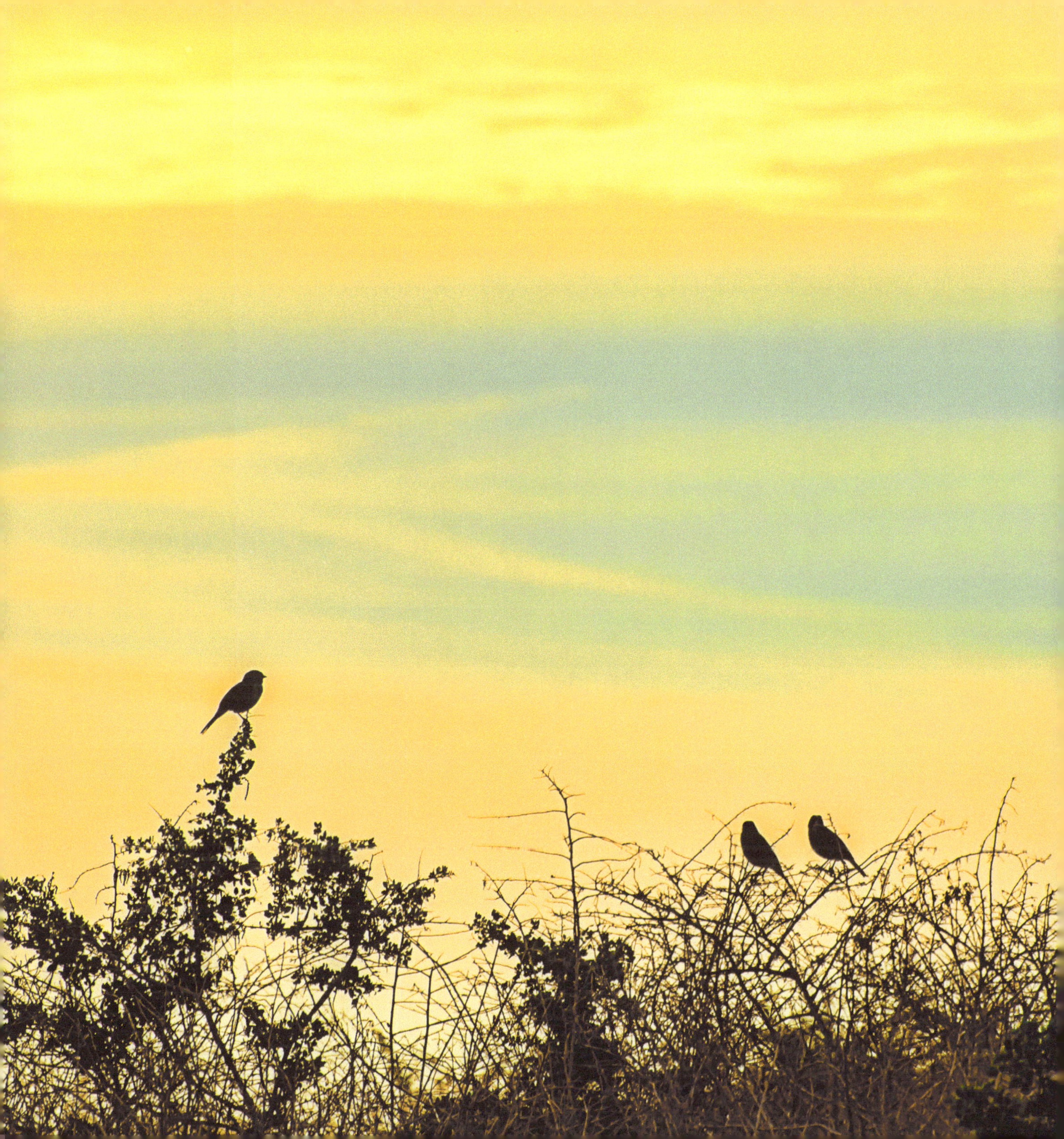

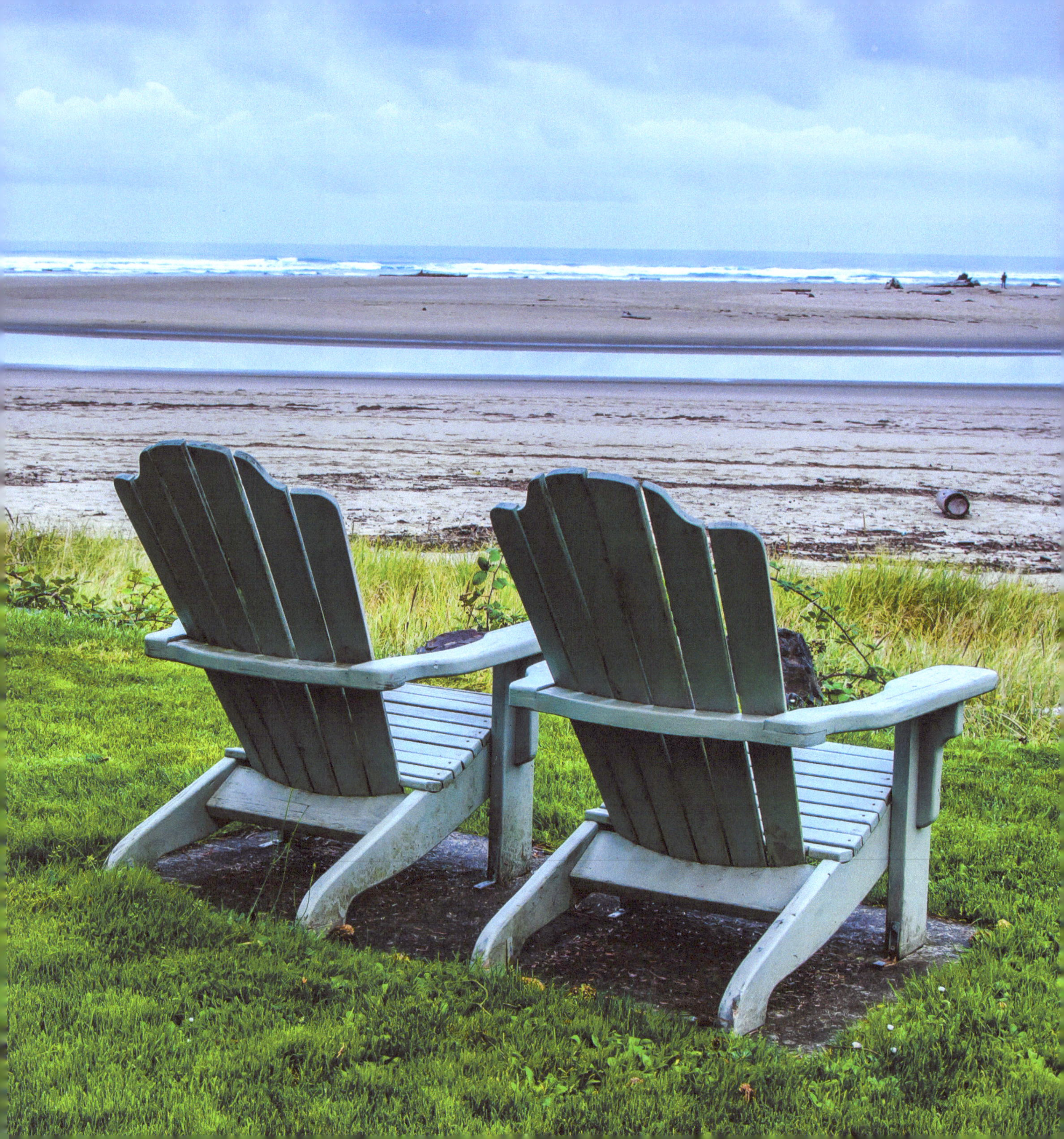

RELATIONSHIP
REFLECTIONS

You Are Intimate with Christ

Therefore, my brethren, you also have become dead to the law through the body of Christ, that you may be married to another—to Him who was raised from the dead, that we should bear fruit to God.

Romans 7:4 NKJV

If you know Christ, then He now lives in you. You are united with Him and in a relationship with Him that is personal and intimate. The more time you spend with Him, the more you will know, love, and trust Him. The Apostle Paul shared his overall goal in life when he said, "I want to know Christ and experience the mighty power that raised him from the dead" (Philippians 3:10 NLT). Your relationship with Christ includes the privilege to walk and talk with Him intimately, moment by moment and day by day. Over time, you will know Him more and more and become like Him. You will grow spiritually and bear much fruit for God.

Lord, thank You that I can know You and that my salvation is not about religion, but a relationship with You. I want to know You more, trust You in every circumstance, and fall more in love with You. In Jesus' Name, Amen.

The Apostle teaches in the fullest form what union with Christ really means. As marriage is the highest form of earthly union, so the spiritual union suggested here transcends every other aspect. Let us ponder this wonderful thought of the believer's union with the Lord Jesus Christ. The penalty of the law has been paid. He has been crucified with Christ, his former connection with the law has gone forever and a new Bridegroom claims his heart as He betroths him to Himself forever.

ROMANS, A DEVOTIONAL COMMENTARY — W.H. GRIFFITH THOMAS

Christ loved the church and gave himself for her to make her holy, cleansing her with the washing of water by the word. He did this to present the church to himself in splendor, without spot or wrinkle or anything like that, but holy and blameless.

EPHESIANS 5:25-27 CSB

Let faith ring these bells of heaven for our joy. Married to Christ. Himself the measure of our responsibilities; Himself the fulness of our capabilities; Himself the possessor of our hearts' affections; Himself the security of our hopes; Himself the well-spring of our fruitfulness; Himself the law of our hearts, our glory, and our crown.

LECTURES ON ROMANS — MARCUS RAINSFORD

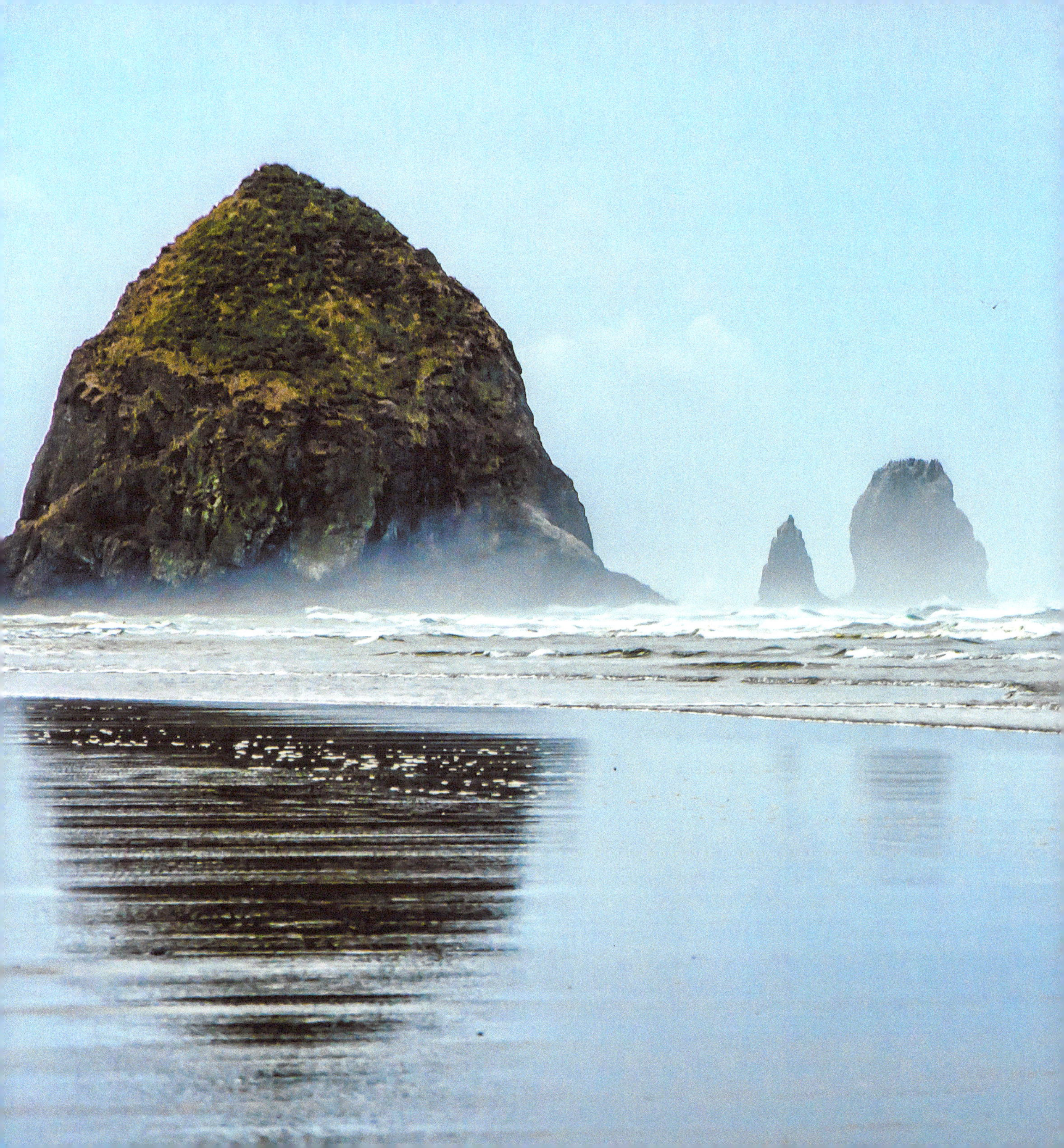

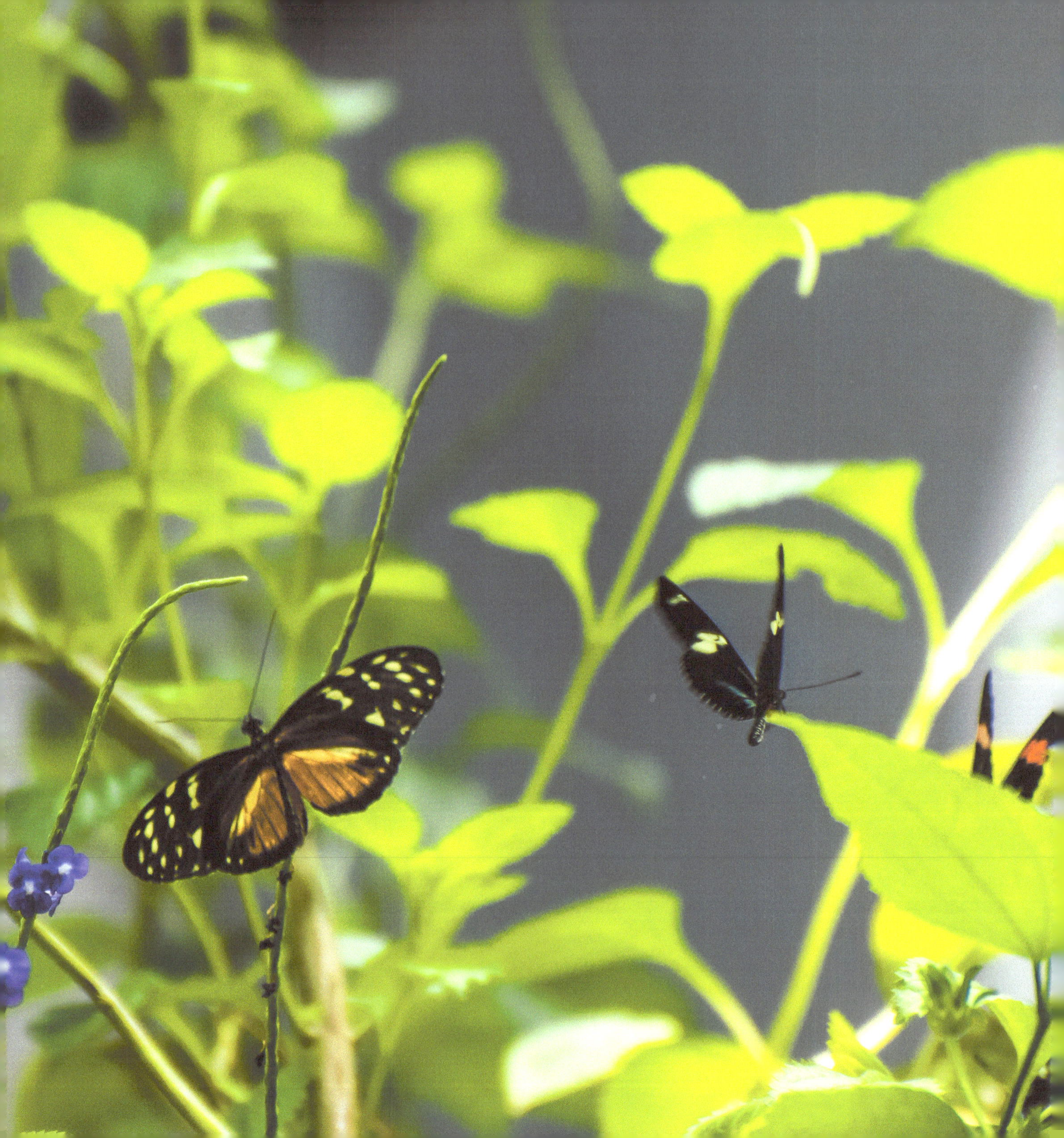

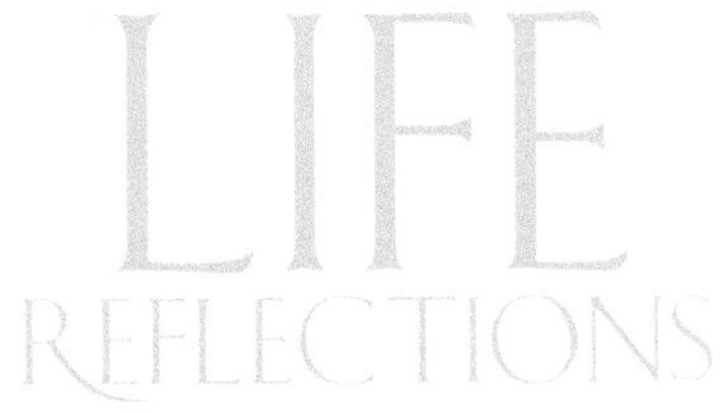

You Experience New Life in Christ

Therefore we have been buried with Him through baptism into death, so that as Christ was raised from the dead through the glory of the Father, so we too might walk in newness of life.
Romans 6:4

If you know Christ, then you will experience a new life in Him. Paul tells us in 2 Corinthians 5:17 that "if anyone is in Christ, he is a new creature; the old things pass away; behold, new things have come." This newness will become apparent when you live a holy life that brings glory to God. Experientially, as we walk in newness of life, we will grow spiritually and our lives will display the life of Christ at work in us as we become more and more like Him. This new life in Christ is eternal, for "the wages of sin is death, but the free gift of God is eternal life in Christ Jesus our Lord" (Romans 6:23).

Lord, thank You giving me a new life, and one that is abundant and lasts forever. I am excited to know You more and become more like You. Teach me Lord and make me the person You want me to be. In Jesus' Name, Amen.

The thief comes only to steal and kill and destroy; I came that they may have life, and have it abundantly.

John 10:10

I stand amazed in the presence of Jesus, the Nazarene
And wonder how He could love me, a sinner, condemned, unclean.

Refrain How marvelous, How wonderful! And my song shall ever be:
How marvelous, How wonderful! Is my Savior's Love for me.

He took my sins and my sorrows; He made them His very own
He bore the burden to Calv'ry and suffered and died alone. Refrain

When with the ransomed in glory His face I at last shall see,
'Twill be my joy thro' the ages to sing of His love for me. Refrain

Charles H. Gabriel, 1905

Since you have been raised to new life with Christ, set your sights on the realities of heaven, where Christ sits in the place of honor at God's right hand. Think about the things of heaven, not the things of earth. For you died to this life, and your real life is hidden with Christ in God. And when Christ, who is your life, is revealed to the whole world, you will share in all his glory.

Colossians 3:1-4 nlt

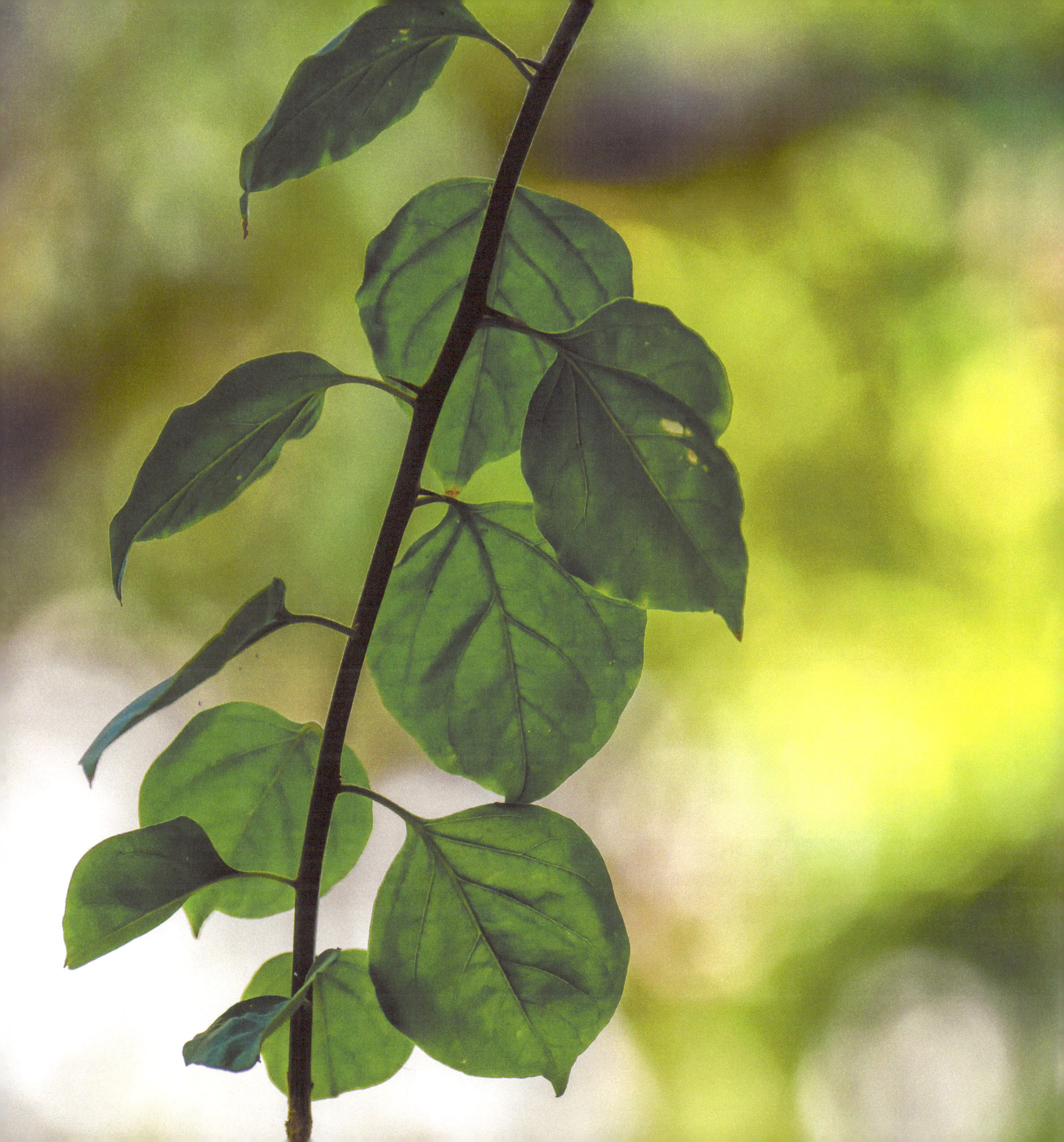

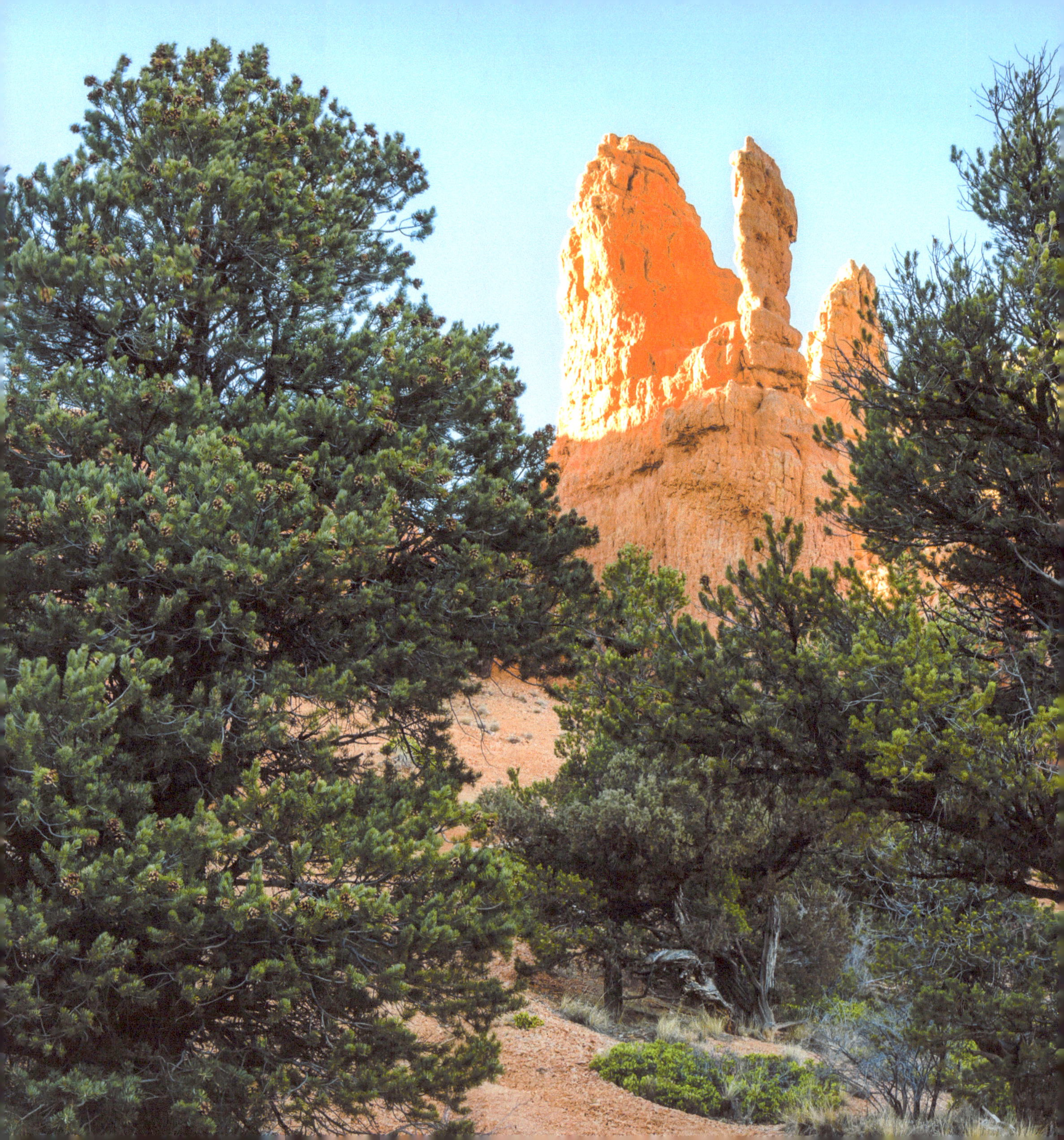

SECURITY
REFLECTIONS

You Are Secure in Christ

As sin reigned in death, even so grace would reign
through righteousness to eternal life through Jesus Christ our Lord.
Romans 5:21

Whoever has the Son of God because of the love of the Father gets it all. You have everything and you have it forever. You are eternally secure. In Romans 5:21 you discover that grace and God's righteousness give you eternal life through Jesus Christ our Lord. What a blessed assurance to know that all we have in Christ lasts forever, extending on into eternity! Dear friend, you can rest your head on the pillow, take a deep breath, and know that because you are now in Christ by grace through faith, you will live forever in heaven with your Lord. You have a future and a hope.

Lord, thank You giving me the assurance of eternal life making me safe and secure forever. Help me always remember Your promises, Your Presence, and Your power contained in the gospel, the good news all about You. In Jesus' Name, Amen.

Therefore there is now no condemnation for those who are in Christ Jesus.

Romans 8:1

Those who are in Christ are not exposed to condemnation. Again, this does not only describe their present state but their permanent position. They are placed beyond the reach of condemnation. They will never be condemned. The meaning of a preposition is often best understood by the arguments by which it is sustained. It is so in this case. The whole chapter (Romans 8) is a proof of the safety of believers, of their security not only from present condemnation but from future perdition. That nothing will ever separate them from the love of God is Paul's triumphant conclusion (Romans 8:35-39).

Romans — Charles Hodge

When you put your faith in Christ, you are joined with Him forever. He is your Bridegroom, Shepherd, Savior, Lord, Rock, Redeemer, Provider, and so much more.

The Proof of God's Amazing Love — Catherine Martin

Give me, my Father, a loving and thankful heart. May your mercies, like cords, bind me to the horns of your altar. Let nothing be held back from you; but may my entire nature be surrendered to your indwelling and service, like a palace in which every room is freely open to its Lord.

Daily Prayers — F.B. Meyer

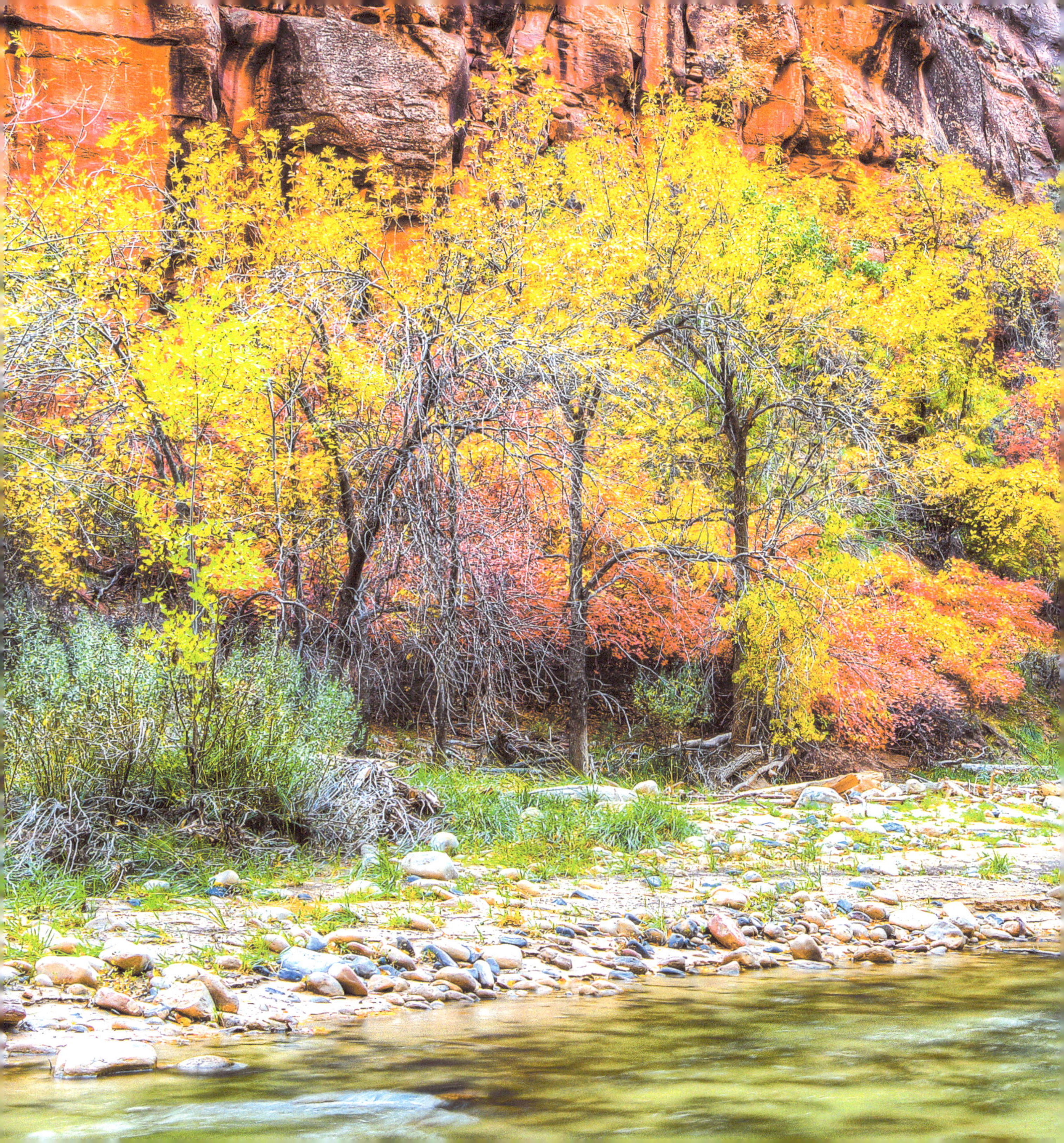

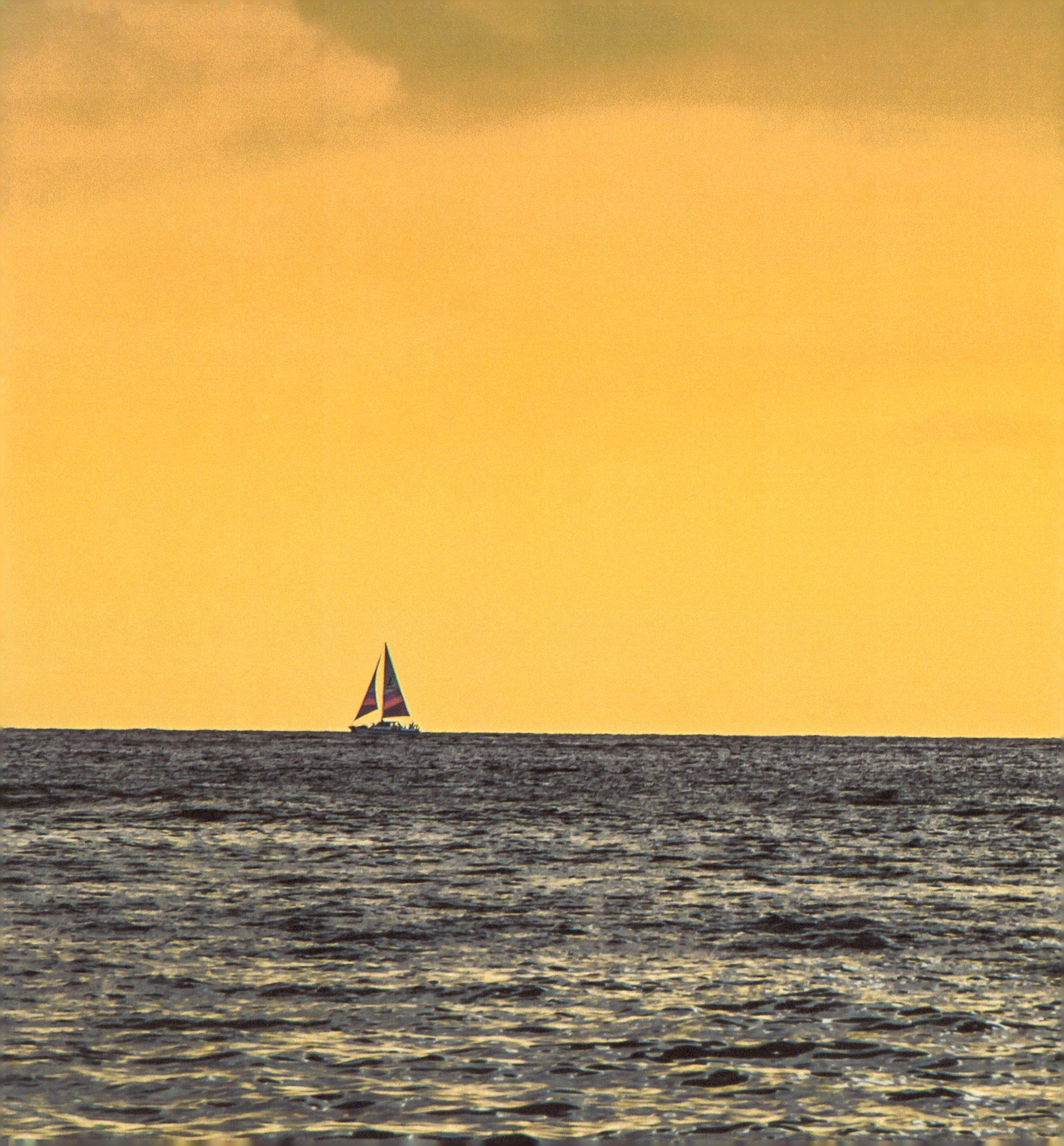

SANCTIFIED
REFLECTIONS

You Are Set Apart in Christ

But now having been freed from sin and enslaved to God, you derive your benefit, resulting in sanctification, and the outcome, eternal life.
Romans 6:22

The benefit of being freed from sin and enslaved to God is sanctification and the outcome is eternal life. Now Paul is showing the wonderful change that takes place. The word translated "sanctification" in the Greek is *hagiasmos* and means holiness, and implies here that we are set aside to God for His holy purposes. We are sanctified (our unchangeable position seen in Hebrews 10:10) and we are being sanctified (the ongoing process of growing spiritually and becoming more like Christ seen in Hebrews 10:14). Sanctification is a great benefit because in it we see progressive spiritual growth and transformation that occur in the life of a believer. The ongoing process of your sanctification will grow through quiet time with God in His Word and prayer.

Lord, thank You for setting me free, sanctifying me, and doing everything necessary to accomplish your purposes and plan in my life. I want to become more and more like Christ, spend quiet time with You, grow in Your grace, and glorify You. In Jesus' Name, Amen.

And so, dear brothers and sisters, I plead with you to give your bodies to God because of all he has done for you. Let them be a living and holy sacrifice—the kind he will find acceptable. This is truly the way to worship him. Don't copy the behavior and customs of this world, but let God transform you into a new person by changing the way you think. Then you will learn to know God's will for you, which is good and pleasing and perfect.

Romans 12:1-2 NLT

It is our privilege to glorify Christ in our body and magnify Christ in our body (Phil. 1:20–21). Just as Jesus Christ had to take on Himself a body in order to accomplish God's will on earth, so we must yield our bodies to Christ that He might continue God's work through us…For many years I have tried to begin each day by surrendering my body to the Lord. Then I spend time with His Word and let Him transform my mind and prepare my thinking for that new day. Then I pray, and I yield the plans of the day to Him and let Him work as He sees best. I especially pray about those tasks that upset or worry me—and He always sees me through. To have a right relationship with God, we must start the day by yielding to Him our bodies, minds, and wills… If you begin each day by surrendering your body to Christ, it will make a great deal of difference in what you do with your body during the day.

Bible Exposition Commentary — Warren Wiersbe

The truths of Romans are transformative, and so it is, when you plumb the depths, you will be transformed by the power of the Holy Spirit. You will be so changed that you will "grow in the grace and knowledge of the Lord Jesus Christ" (2 Peter 3:18), and you will serve Him well bringing great glory and honor to Him.

The Proof of God's Amazing Love — Catherine Martin

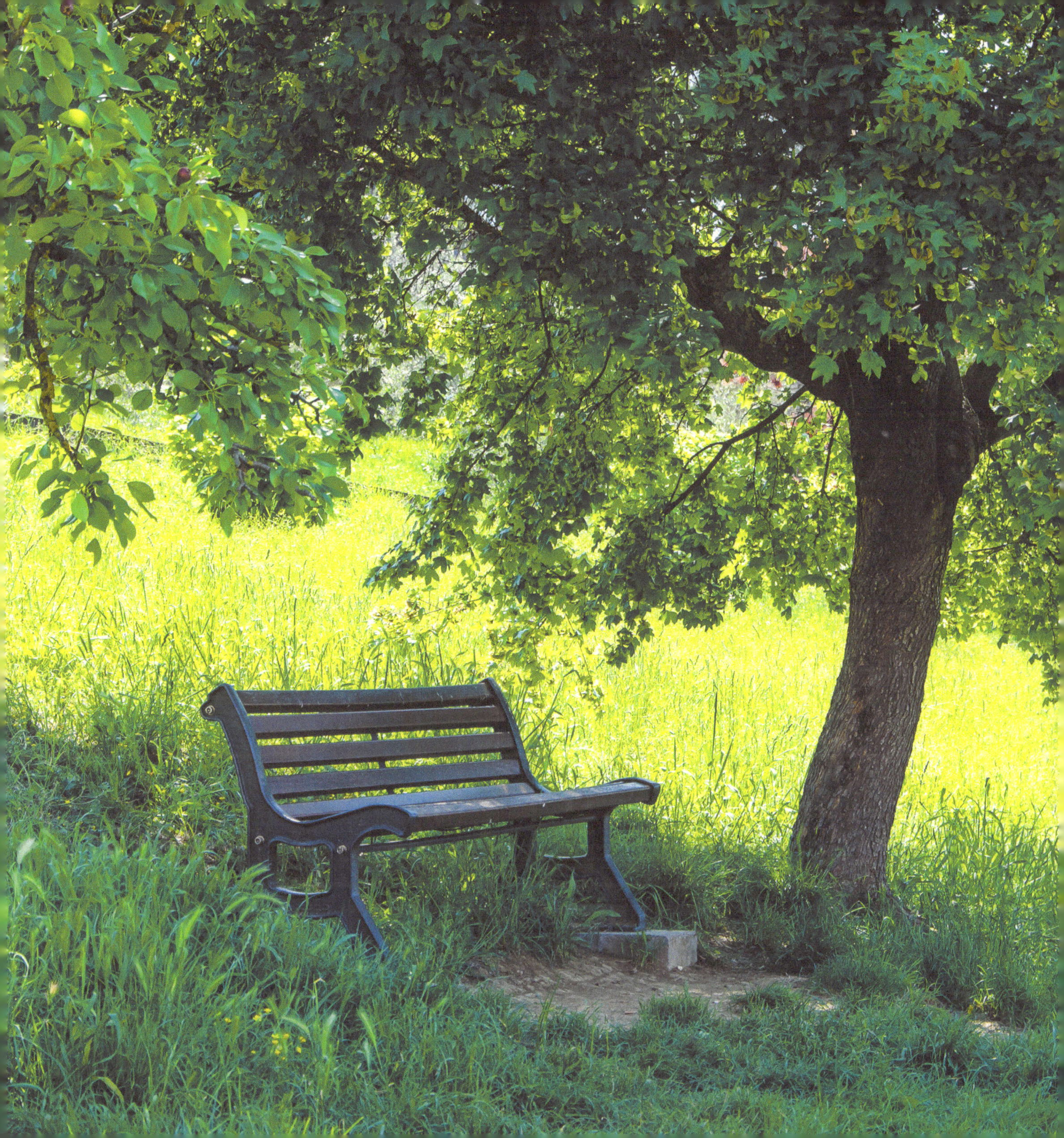

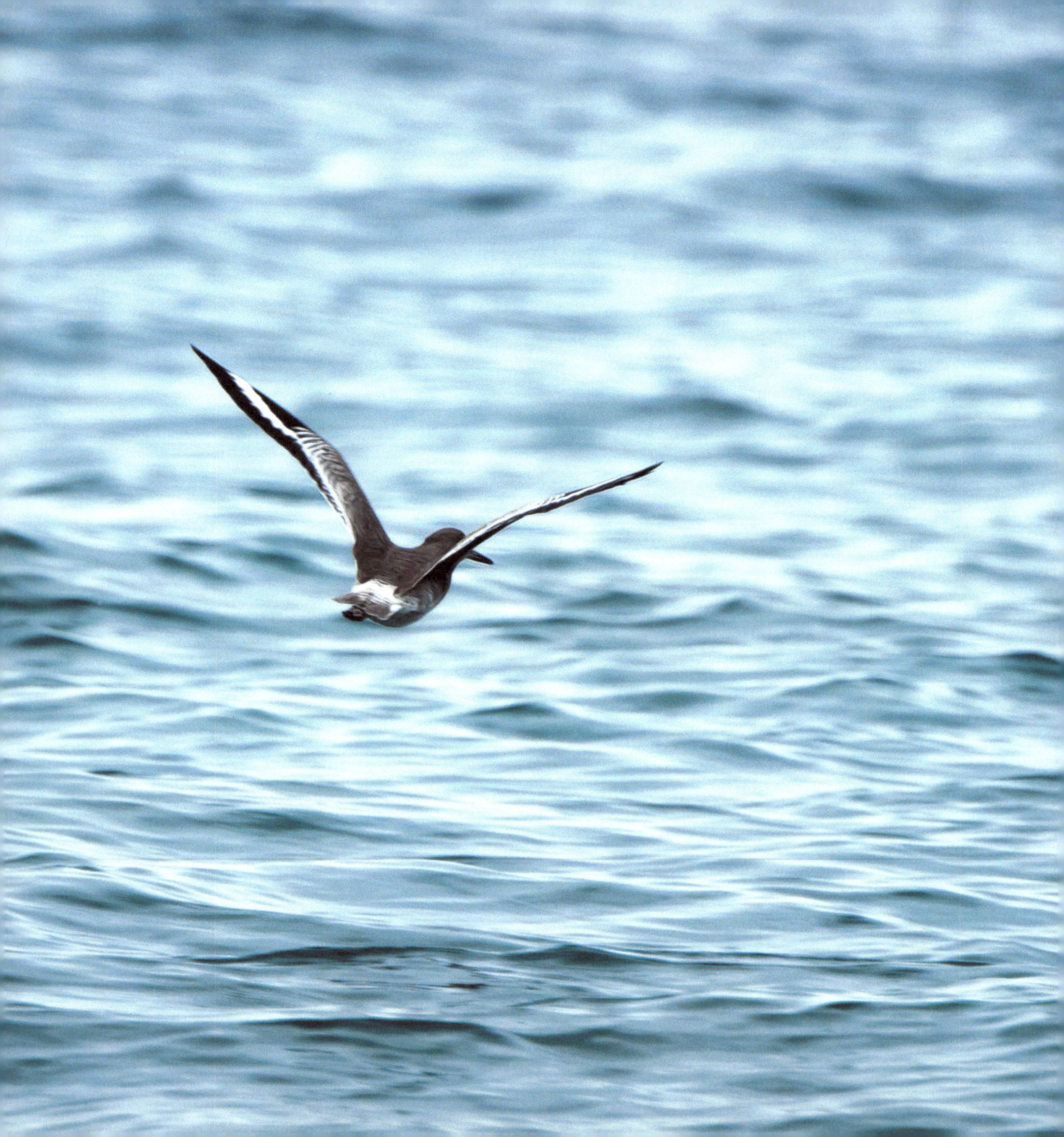

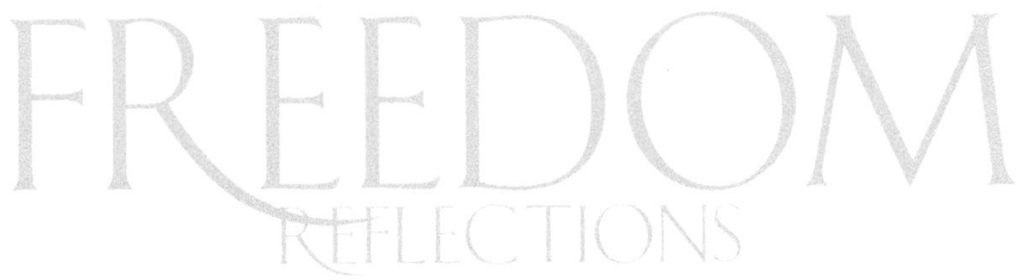

You Are Set Free in Christ

Our old self was crucified with Him, in order that our body of sin might be done away with, so that we would no longer be slaves to sin, for he who has died is freed from sin.
Romans 6:6-7

You are set free. Being "freed from sin" means we are acquitted. There is a difference that has now taken place because of Christ. We are now slaves of righteousness (Romans 6:18) and we live "to God" because of our union with Christ and our identification with Him (Romans 6:10). Now Paul is showing a great change that has taken place in who you are and Whose you are. You are not meant for the immorality of this world; you are like an eagle, set free to soar the heights with your Lord. And you can know this: "If the Son makes you free, you will be free indeed" (John 8:36).

Lord, thank You for freeing me from sin and death so I might live for You. I now belong to You. Help me live like an eagle and soar the heights with You. In Jesus' Name, Amen.

A Texas rancher, hunting in the mountains, came upon an eagle's nest, and took one of the eggs back home with him, and placed it under a setting hen. The eagle was hatched and cared for by the mother hen. For some period of time, the eagle seemed perfectly content to remain in the barnyard and feed along with the chickens. That is, until it heard the harsh scream of a mature eagle, swooping down in search of prey. In the blink of an eye, the young eagle ascended into the sky and was never seen again. It had found its new home in the mountainside cliffs, for that young eagle was not made for the barnyard dirt but meant to soar in the heights above.

The Proof of God's Amazing Love — Catherine Martin

For the law of the Spirit of life in Christ Jesus has set you free from the law of sin and death.

Romans 8:2

The power of sin in our lives is broken because Christ has set us free. We are now united with Christ. We are no longer under the Law but under grace. Yours is an unchangeable and unshakeable position in Christ. You are forever secure in Christ. It means that presenting ourselves to the Law and making resolutions and vows doesn't help us live to God and righteousness. What it does mean is that united with Christ, and living in His power, we now are set free to actually resist sin and say "no" to sin as we present our members to God in the power of the Holy Spirit. Liberty and freedom are never a license to sin. Experientially, as we walk in newness of life, we will grow spiritually and our lives will display the life of Christ at work in us as we become more and more like Him.

The Proof of God's Amazing Love — Catherine Martin

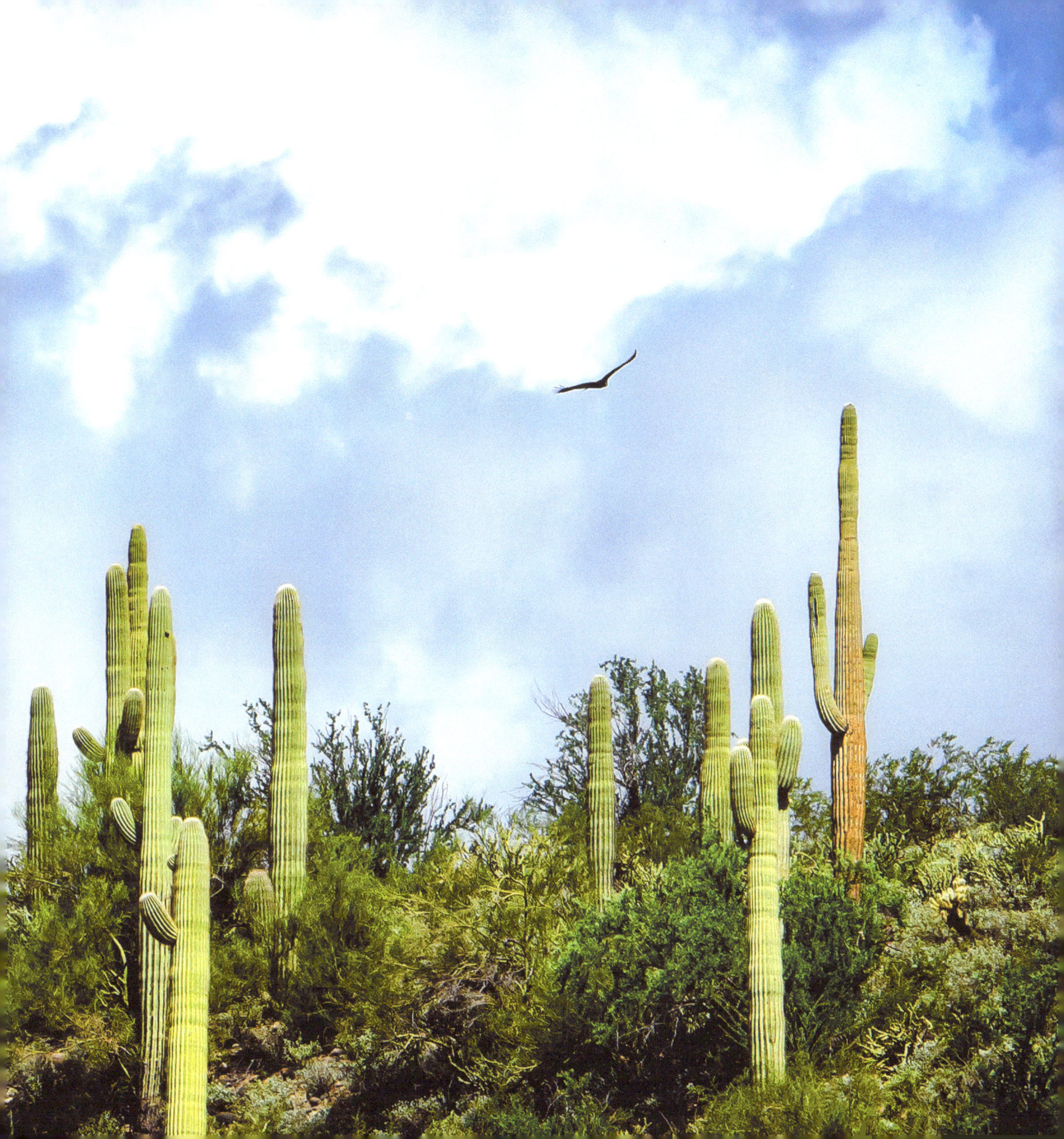

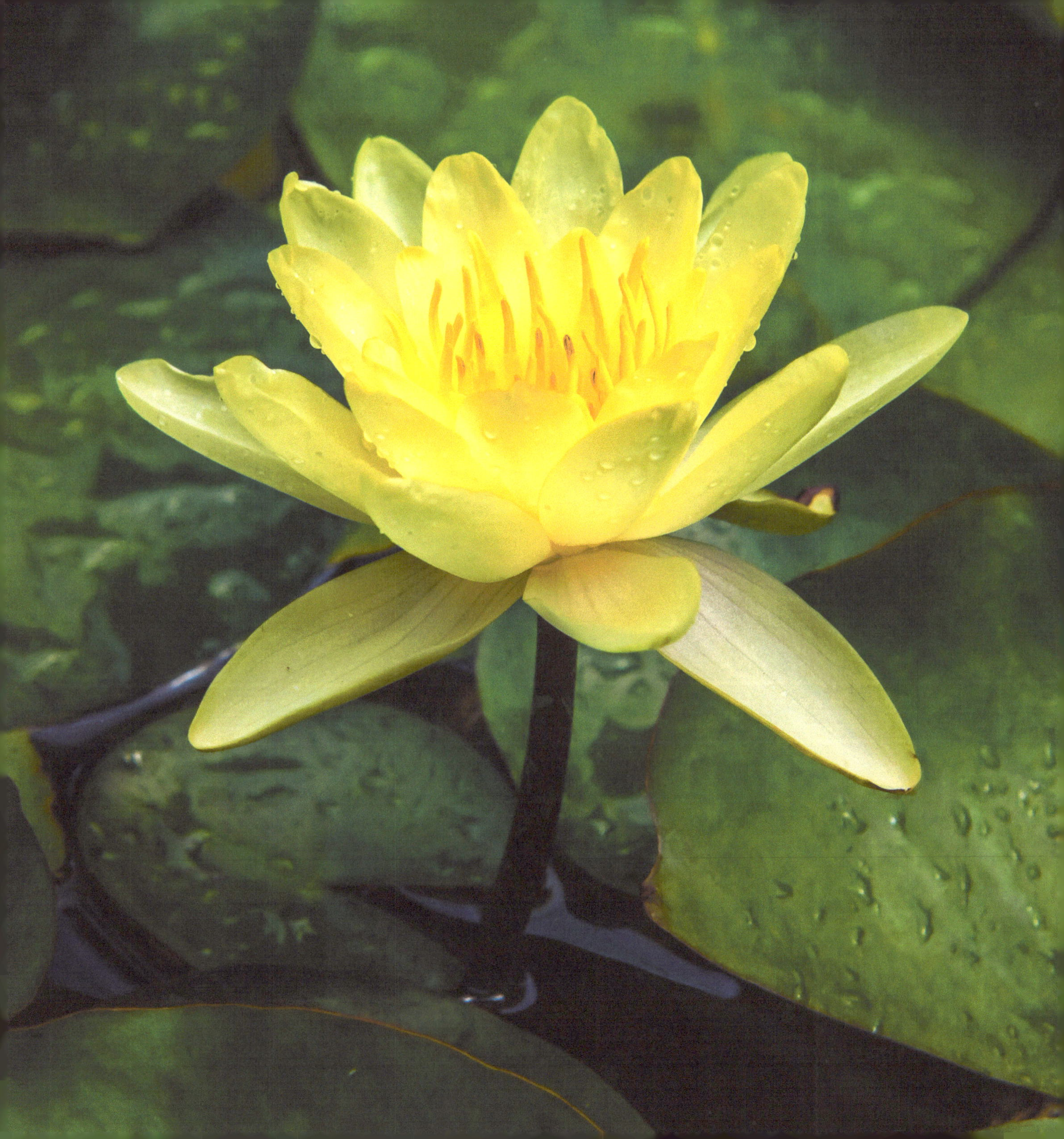

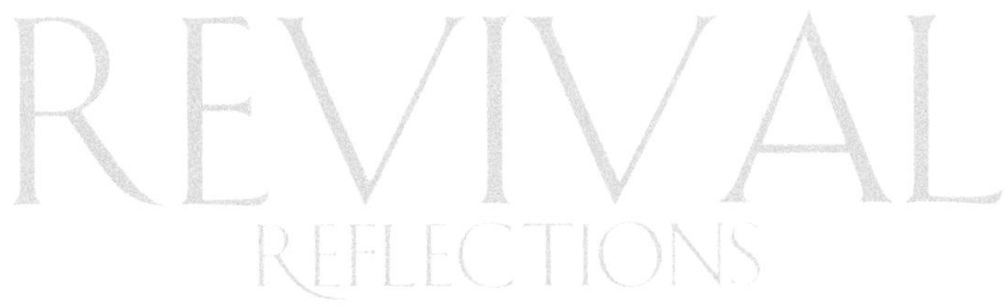

You Experience Revival in Christ

You are not in the flesh, but in the Spirit, if indeed the Spirit of God dwells in you…if Christ is in you, though the body is dead because of sin, yet the spirit is alive because of righteousness.
Romans 8:9-10

Once you are saved, you are indwelt by the Holy Spirit and the power of God is now present and working in you. God wants to start a revival and He does it beginning with you through the power of the Holy Spirit. Personal spiritual revival is a quickening of heart and soul by God, imparting whatever is necessary to sustain one's spiritual life and enable a return to the experience of one's true purpose as ordained by God. And how are we revived? By God, through His Word, in the power of the Holy Spirit. You enjoy and experience life in Christ and all His benefits moment by moment through the Holy Spirit.

Lord, start a revival in me through the Holy Spirit who lives in me. I want to know and love You more today and live out Your plan and purpose for me. In Jesus' Name, Amen.

Revival commences with those who in bad times remain good, in godless days remain Christian, in careless years remain constant and who have eternity in their hearts. …Revival is always a personal thing, and no one is used in revival who is not himself revived first. That is very important to understand. Those whom God uses in leadership in revival are always men who have met with God in a powerfully personal way and have a burning passion for the glory of God and a life of holiness.

Revival: A People Saturated With God — Brian H. Edwards

Give me Thy strength for my day, Lord
That whereso'er I go,
There shall no danger daunt me and I shall fear no foe;
So shall no task o'ercome me, So shall not trial fret,
So shall I walk unwearied the path where my feet are set;
So shall I find no burden greater than I can bear,
So shall I have a courage equal to all my care;
So shall no grief o'erwhelm me, So shall no wave o'erflow;
Give me Thy strength for my day, Lord,
Cover my weakness so.

Annie Johnson Flint

A spiritual person, then, is one who experiences the divine purpose and plan in his daily life through the power of the indwelling Spirit. The character of that life will be the out-lived Christ. The cause of that life will be the unhindered indwelling Spirit (Ephesians 3:16-21, 2 Corinthians 3:18).

He That Is Spiritual — Lewis Sperry Chafer

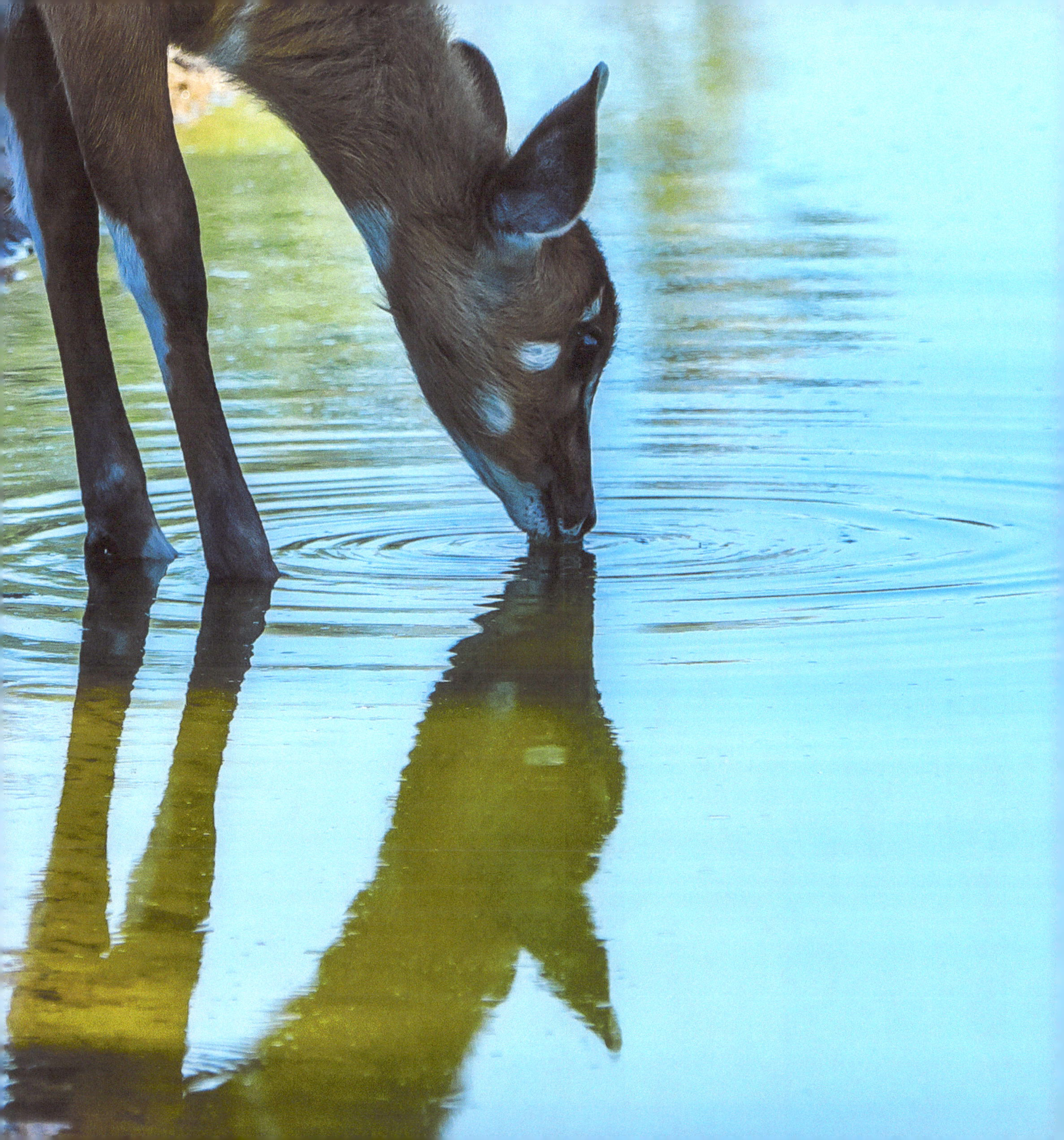

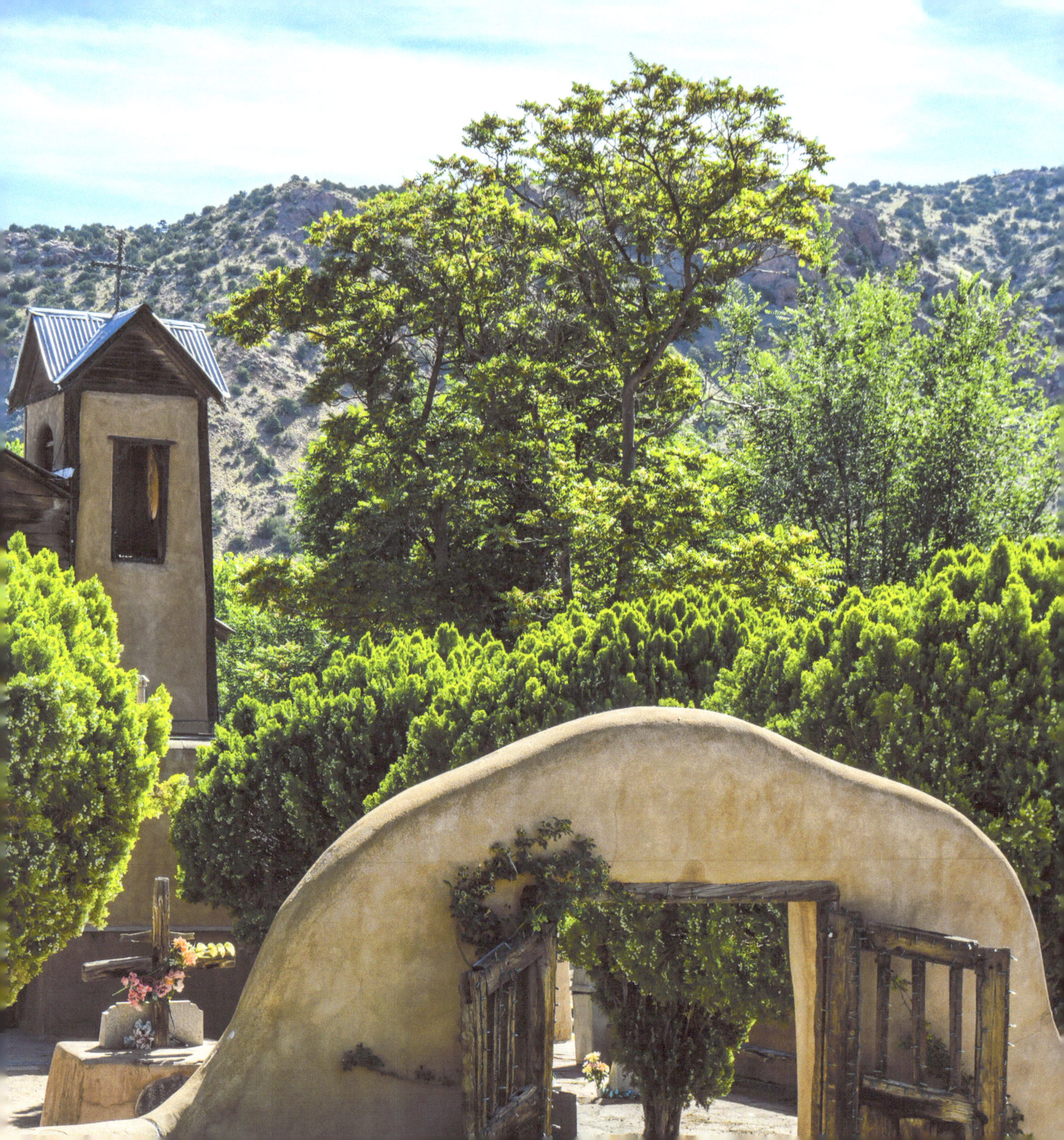

PRAYER
REFLECTIONS

You Experience Power In Prayer

In the same way the Spirit also helps our weakness; for we do not know how to pray as we should, but the Spirit Himself intercedes with groanings too deep for words…
Romans 8:26

Have you ever felt as though you didn't know what to pray or how to pray? God has given you help for all your prayers. The Spirit Himself intercedes for us with groanings too deep for words according to the will of God (Romans 8:26-27) and Christ also intercedes for us (Romans 8:34). Additional help in prayer comes with all God's promises, a sure foundation for they reveal to us God's will and God's ways. God has given you powerful prayer partners and all His promises resulting in His power as you pray. You will experience the thrill of watching God do great and mighty things in your life when you pray.

Lord, thank You for giving me a wonderful life of prayer through the power of the Holy Spirit. Help me discover Your promises and pray believing Your Word. In Jesus' Name, Amen.

Lord, teach us to pray. Some of us are not skilled in the art of prayer. As we draw near to Thee in thought, our spirits long for Thy Spirit, and reach out for Thee, longing to feel Thee near. We know not how to express the deepest emotions that lie hidden in our hearts… give us the vision, the courage, that shall enlarge our horizons and stretch our faith to the adventure of seeking Thy loving will for our lives. We thank Thee that Thou art hearing us even now. We thank Thee for the grace of prayer. We thank Thee for Thyself. Amen.

The Prayers of Peter Marshall — Catherine Marshall

Don't worry about anything; instead, pray about everything. Tell God what you need, and thank him for all he has done. Then you will experience God's peace, which exceeds anything we can understand. His peace will guard your hearts and minds as you live in Christ Jesus.

Philippians 4:6-7 NLT

Catherine Marshall was an American author and the wife of Peter Marshall, a well known Presbyterian minister and Chaplain of the U.S. Senate. In her book, *Beyond Ourselves*, she shares the story of how the Lord worked in her life during a time of suffering. She had been ill for six months with a lung infection. In spite of evaluations by many specialists, nothing seemed to help, and she was bedridden full-time. She came to a place where she surrendered to the will of God in a new and deeper way and prayed: "I'm beaten, God. You decide what You want for me." She sensed Christ with her and experienced revitalized faith and trust in Him, no matter what happened. Her recovery began from that moment. She called it the Prayer of Relinquishment where she voluntarily gave up her self-will to God, with no demands of Him, only trust for His will, His way. And in time, Catherine fully recovered from her illness.

The Proof of God's Amazing Love — Catherine Martin

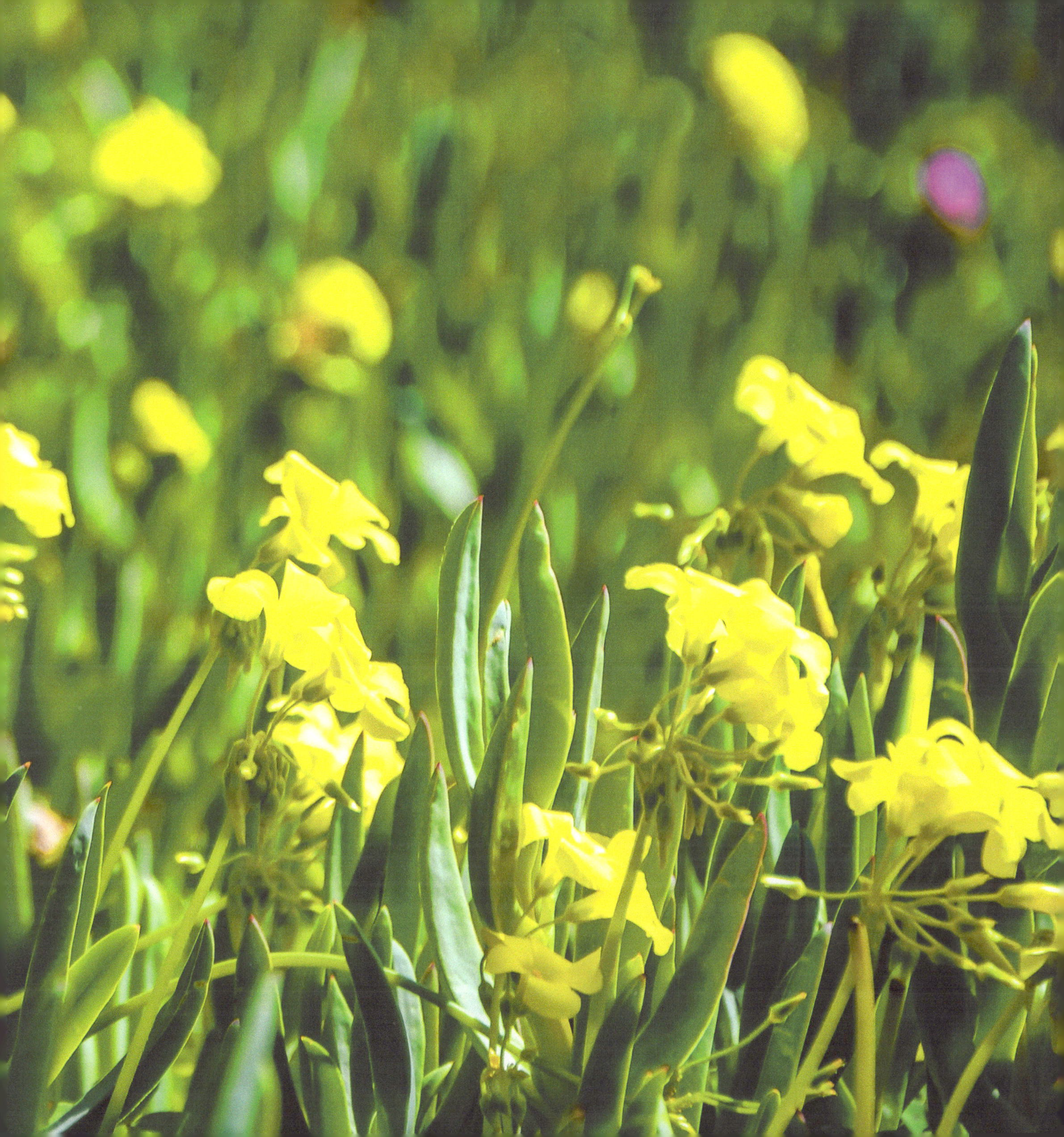

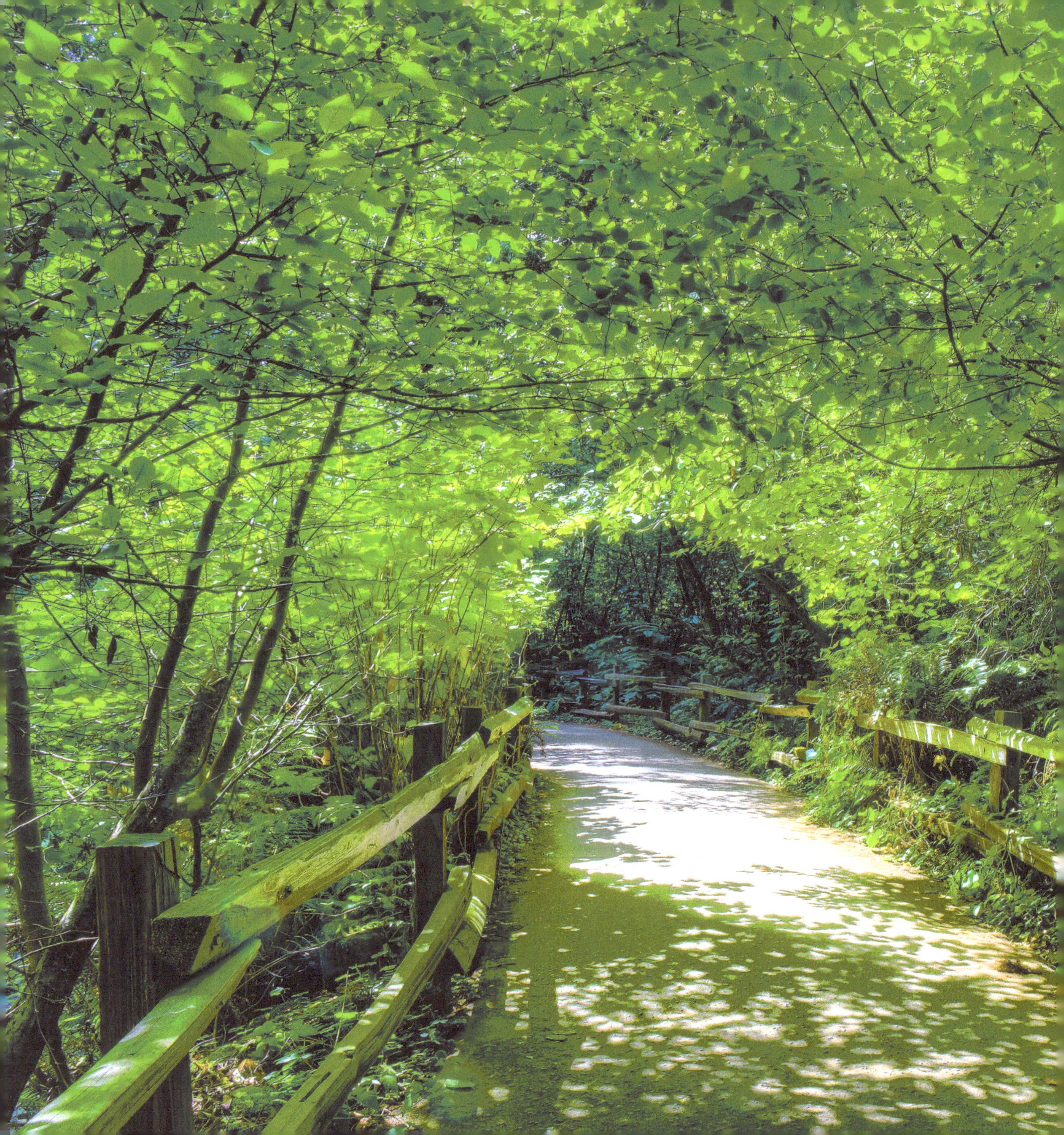

GUIDANCE
REFLECTIONS

You Are Led by the Holy Spirit

For all who are being led by the Spirit of God, these are sons of God.
Romans 8:14

Your life in Christ carries the promise of guidance through life. As a child of God, you are "being led by the Spirit of God" (Romans 8:14). Guidance relies on the One leading, and you can count on your Lord as you walk by faith in life. One way to remember the meaning of G-U-I-DANCE is *God, You and I Dance.* When you lean into your Lord's embrace and follow His lead, you will dance. Only one can lead in the dance and the more you surrender to Him, the more you will experience His guidance in life. Always remember that those who walk with God always get to their destination.

Lord, help me surrender to You and lean into Your embrace as You lead me in life. I want to dance with You. In Jesus' Name, Amen.

Faith never knows where it is being led, but it loves and knows the One Who is leading. It is a life of faith, not of intellect and reason, but a life of knowing Who makes us 'go'. The root of faith is the knowledge of a Person.

My Utmost for His Highest — Oswald Chambers

Teach me to do your will, for you are my God.
May your gracious Spirit lead me forward on a firm footing.

Psalm 143:10 NLT

These men [the disciples and their ministry seen in Acts] learned to live always in the presence of a Jesus whom their outer eyes saw not…He would be with them continually manifesting Himself in rarest power of action, in tenderest personal care, in talking and walking with them. They would see the power plainly at work; then they would say in a soft hush, He is here. They would find new bodily strength, new guidance in perplexity, new peace in the midst of confusion, and they would say to each other in awed tones, He is here: it's the Master's touch. And so it would come to be a habit to anticipate His presence. They would figure Him in, and figure Him in big, as big as He is, in all sorts of circumstances and planning and meeting of difficulties.

Quiet Talks On John's Gospel — S.D. Gordon

Since we live by the Spirit, let us keep in step with the Spirit.

Galatians 5:25 NIV

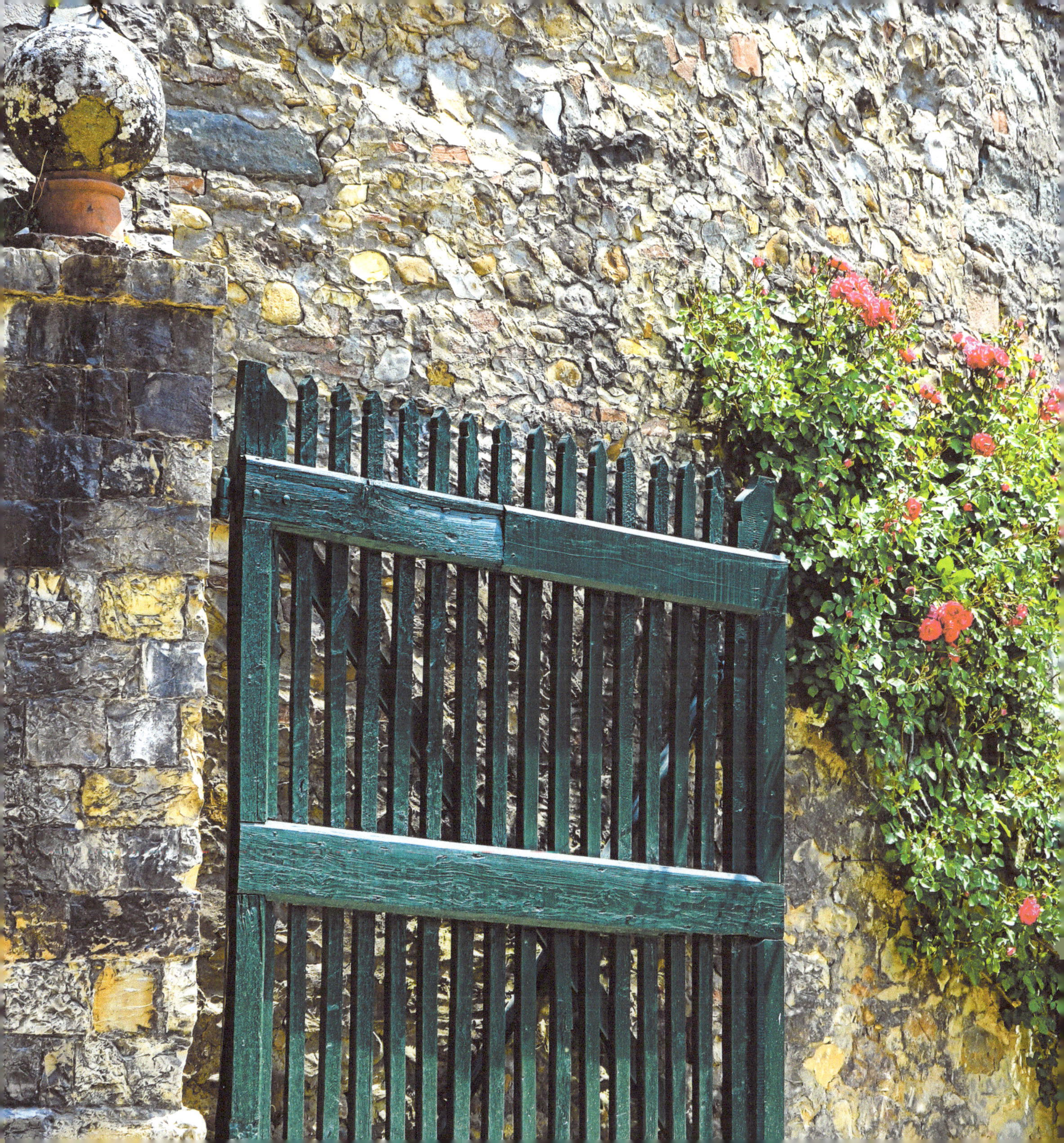

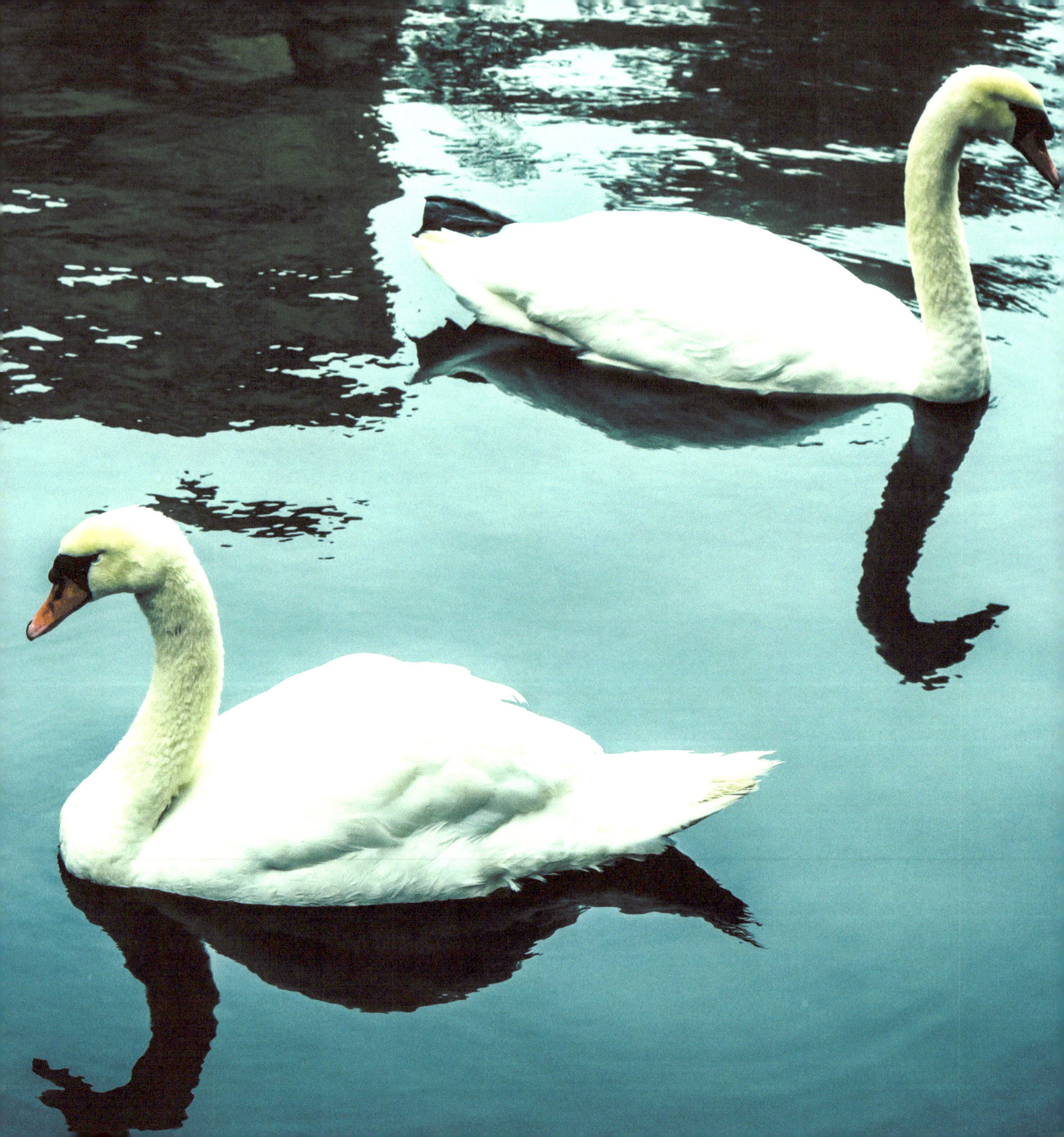

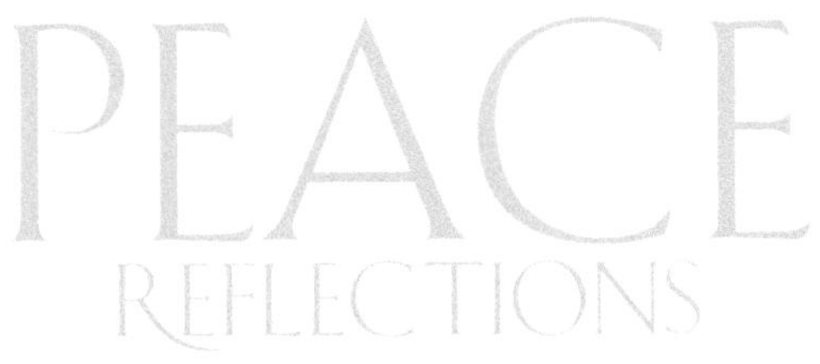

You Experience Peace with God

Therefore having been justified by faith, we have peace with God through our Lord Jesus Christ.
Romans 5:1

Having been justified by faith (pardoned, acquitted, declared righteous), you now have peace with God. This phrase has been described as sitting down in one's heart with God and experiencing gladness in being with Him. What a beautiful picture of the relationship that is now ours with God because of Christ. You are in the unshakeable position of having moved forever from enmity to friendship, and from hostility to peace and divine favor. When you experience peace with God, you will know the peace of God more and more—a tranquil soul assured of salvation—through the power of the Holy Spirit as you daily walk by faith.

Lord, thank You for placing me in this unshakeable position of peace with You. I trust in You today for Your peace as I sit down with You in my heart. In Jesus' Name, Amen.

How does God touch our hearts? Our heavenly Father generally uses a soft, tender, gentle, quiet, calm, and peaceful—still, small—voice. Softly and gently, the Holy Spirit works like the breath of spring dissolving icebergs and melting glaciers. After winter has taken every stream by the throat and held it fast, spring sets it free. No hammer or file is heard as the icy bonds fall off; only the soft south wind blows, and all is life and liberty. So it is with the work of the Holy Spirit when He comes into the soul. He can be a mighty rushing wind (Acts 2:2), for He comes according to His own sovereign pleasure. Yet when He brings the peace of God, He usually descends as the dove (Matt. 3:16) or as the dew from heaven—all peace, all gentle, and all quiet.

Beside Still Waters — Charles Haddon Spurgeon

For the mind set on the flesh is death, but the mind set on the Spirit is life and peace.

Romans 8:6

None can be lost who take Jesus as the door of faith to their souls. Entrance through Jesus into peace is the guarantee of entrance by the same door into heaven. Jesus is the only door, an open door, a wide door, a safe door; and blessed is he who rests all his hope of admission to glory upon the crucified Redeemer.

Charles Haddon Spurgeon

For the kingdom of God is not a matter of eating and drinking, but
of righteousness, peace and joy in the Holy Spirit.

Romans 14:17

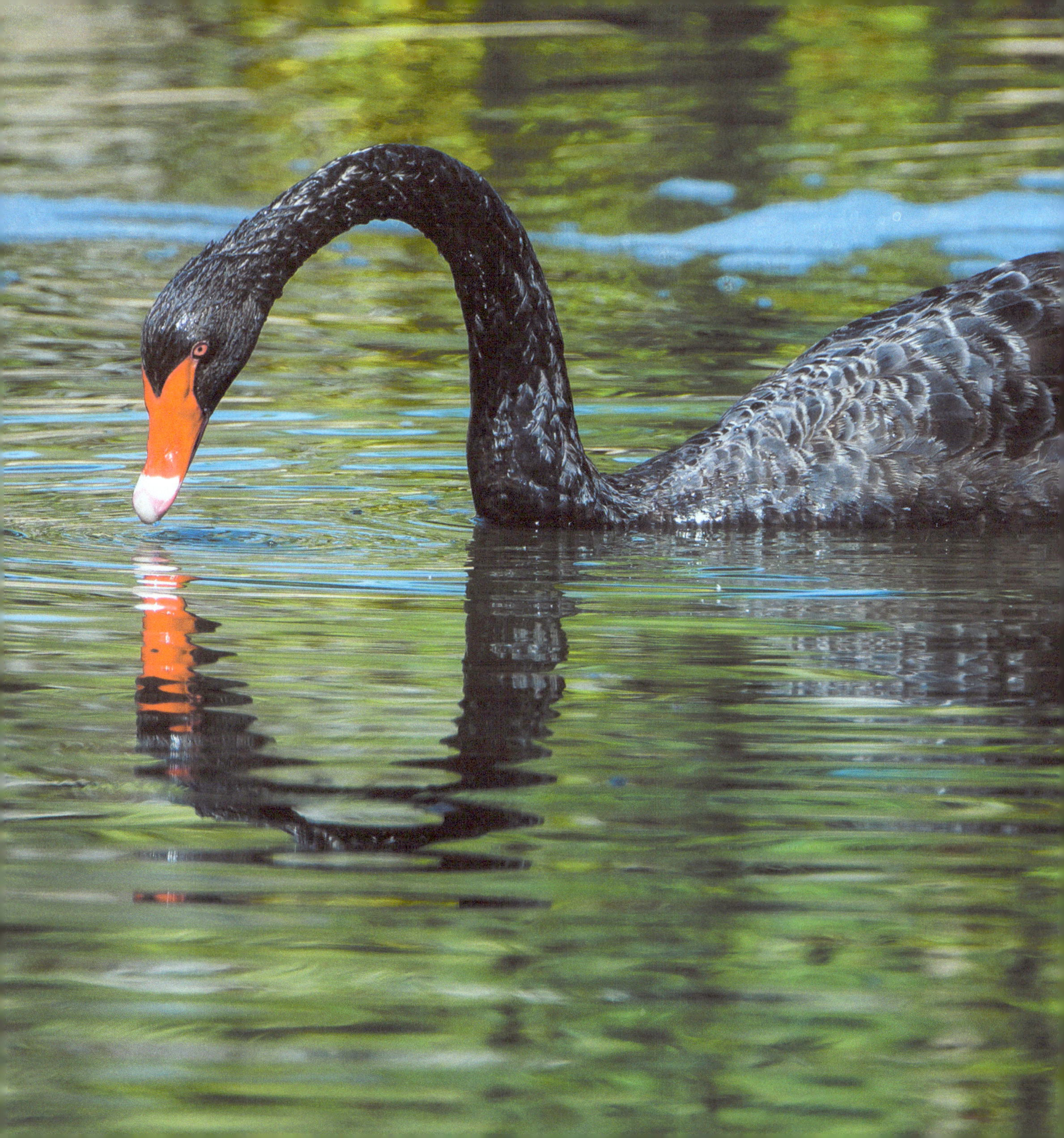

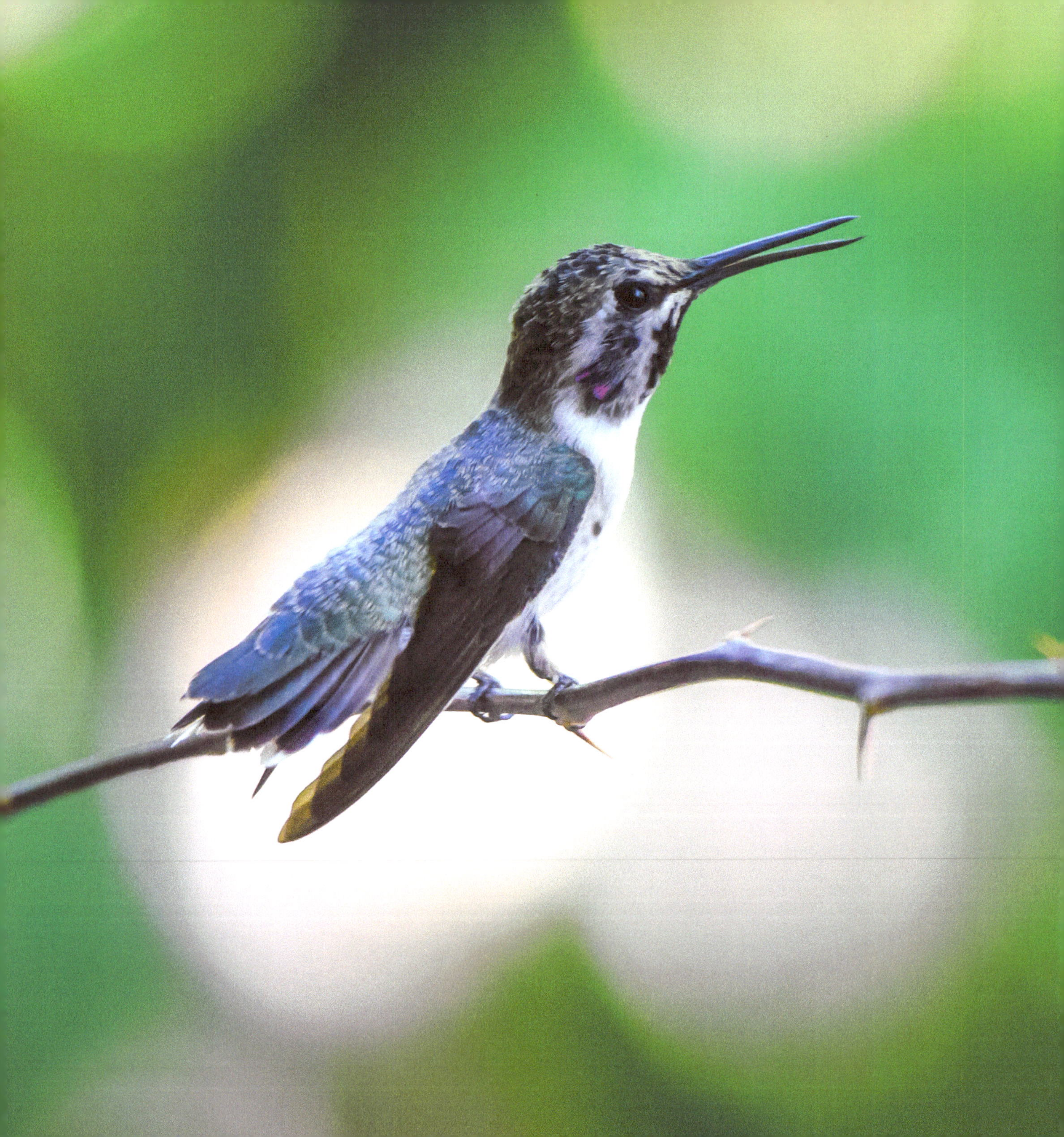

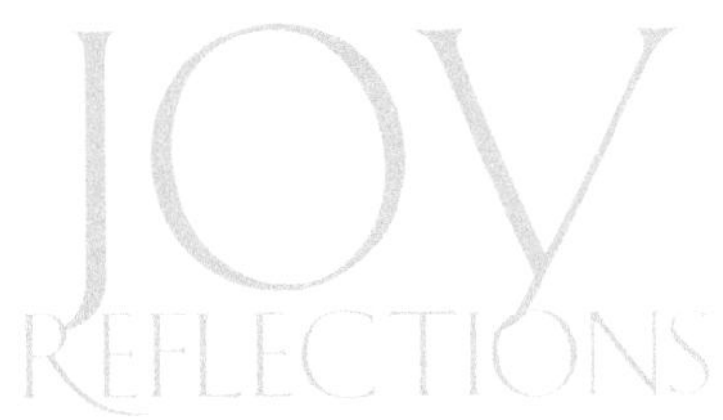

You Are Filled With Joy

Now may the God of hope fill you with all joy and peace in believing…
Romans 15:13

When the Lord Jesus lives in you, you are changed, transformed, and you act differently in all kinds of situations. You will be different even as you live in the world of governments and nations, different with your neighbors, and different in your own lifestyle. You will live a life of hope and encouragement, and joy and peace as you are conformed to the image of Christ in the power of the Holy Spirit. The joy of the Lord will be your strength (Nehemiah 8:10). It has been said that joy is not the absence of suffering but the presence of God. His joy will make you shine with the love of Jesus Christ.

Lord, thank You for filling me with Your joy even in times of difficulty. Fill me with the Holy Spirit that I may know and love You more. In Jesus' Name, Amen.

I am coming to you now, but I say these things while I am still in the world, so that they may have the full measure of my joy within them.

The Prayer of Jesus — John 17:13 niv

Paul spoke from the white-hot conviction that is born of experience. On the road to Damascus, he had in a single instant all the artificial props of works, race and character knocked out from under him. He caught a full glimpse of the glorified Christ. From then on, he had but one message: faith in the crucified and risen Lord. He would hear nothing else; he spoke nothing else; he lived nothing less…Paul was proud of the gospel because he had proved its power in his own life and in the lives of all who would believe…Romans is Paul's shout of joy to a lost world.

What the Bible is All About — Henrietta C. Mears

I listened to the Word of God; and that precious text led me to the cross of Christ. I can testify that the joy of that day was utterly indescribable. I could have leaped, I could have danced; there was no expression, however fanatical, which would have been out of keeping with the joy of my spirit at that hour… I felt that I was an emancipated soul, an heir of Heaven, a forgiven one, accepted in Christ Jesus,

The Autobiography of Spurgeon — Charles Haddon Spurgeon

Let me turn to you, O Lord, from the sweetest of earthly joys, to find that you are best of all, the fairest among ten thousand, and altogether lovely.

Daily Prayers — F.B. Meyer

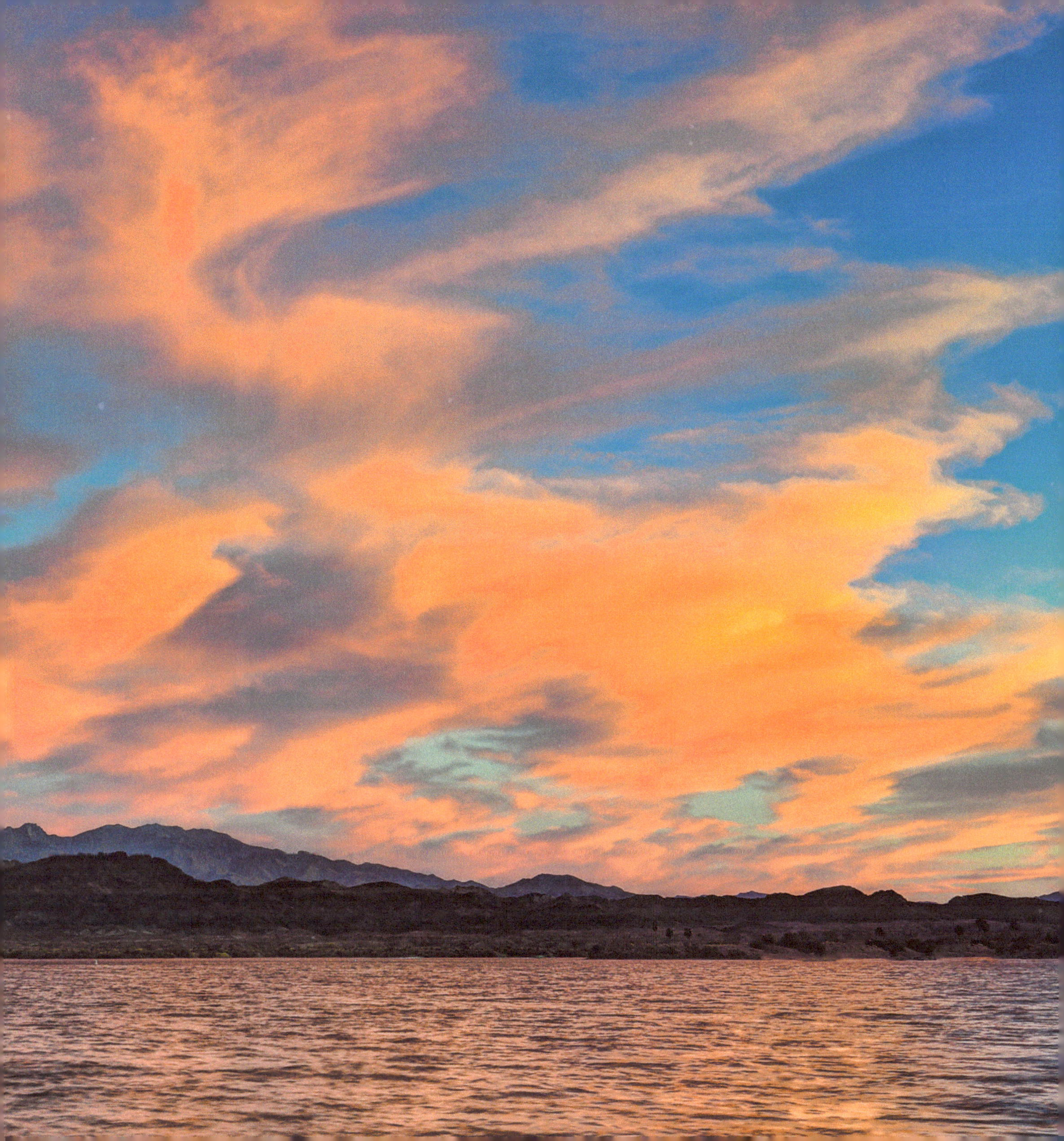

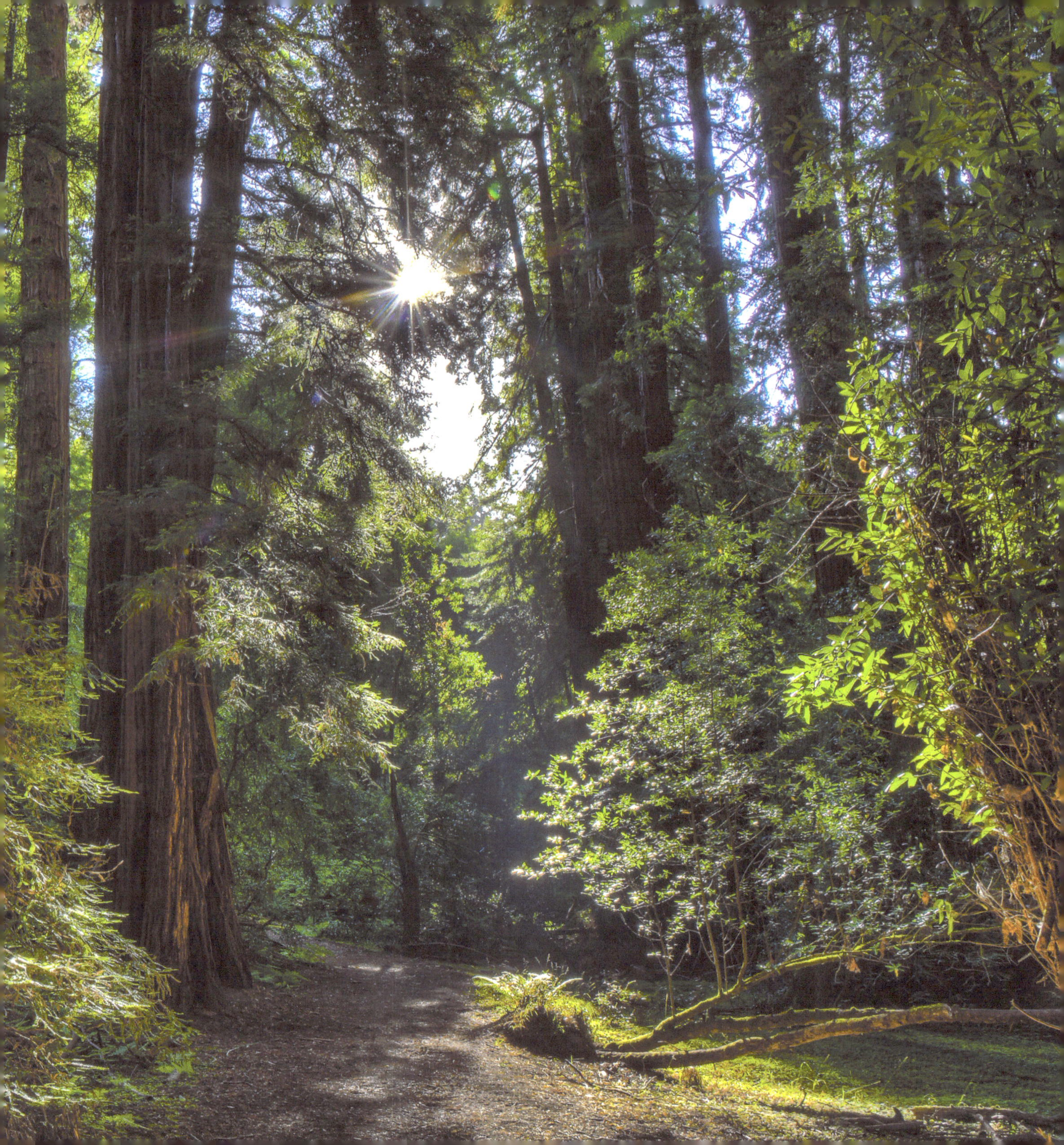

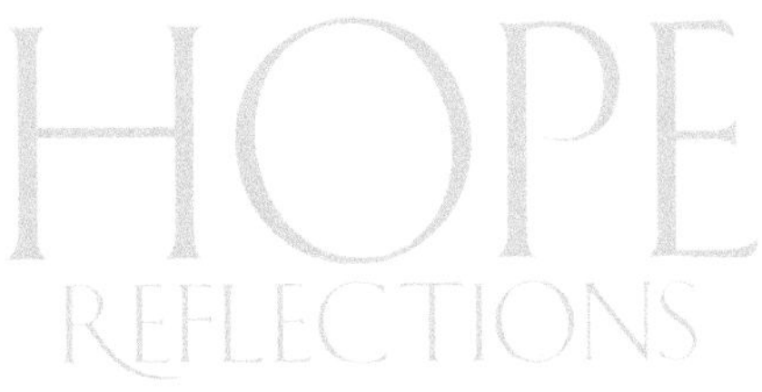

You Always Have Hope

...you will abound in hope by the power of the Holy Spirit.
Romans 15:13

The gospel's power in us is seen in a prominent distinguishing characteristic for the just people who live by faith. They have hope. In fact, sometimes those around us may wonder how we can possibly keep going or have a smile with such adversity in our lives. What Paul shares in Romans 15:13 is that we "abound in hope by the power of the Holy Spirit." The indwelling Holy Spirit does in us what we can never do for ourselves. He gives us hope. Hope is the crowning glory for every child of God. It is why a suffering Christian shines as a light in the world. H-O-P-E is *Holding On with Patient Expectation.*

Lord, thank You for giving me hope even in the impossibles of my life. Help me hold on with patient expectation today. In Jesus' Name, Amen.

For whatever was written in earlier times was written for our instruction, so that through perseverance and the encouragement of the Scriptures we might have hope.

Romans 15:4

Have we not known men whose lives have not given out any entrancing music in the day of a calm prosperity, but who, when the tempest drove against them, have astonished their fellows by the power and strength of their music?

The Silver Lining — John Henry Jowett

There is never a time when we may not hope in God. Whatever our necessities, however great our difficulties, and though to all appearance help is impossible, yet our business is to hope in God, and it will be found that it is not in vain. In the Lord's own time help will come. Oh, the hundreds, yea, the thousands of times that I have found it thus within the past seventy years and four months! When it seemed impossible that help could come, help did come; for God has His own resources. He is not confined. In ten thousand different ways, and at ten thousand different times God may help us. Our business is to spread our cases before the Lord, in childlike simplicity to pour out all our heart before God…I continually say to myself, "Hope thou in God."

Streams in the Desert — George Mueller

"For I know the plans that I have for you," declares the Lord, "plans for welfare and not for calamity to give you a future and a hope."

Jeremiah 29:11

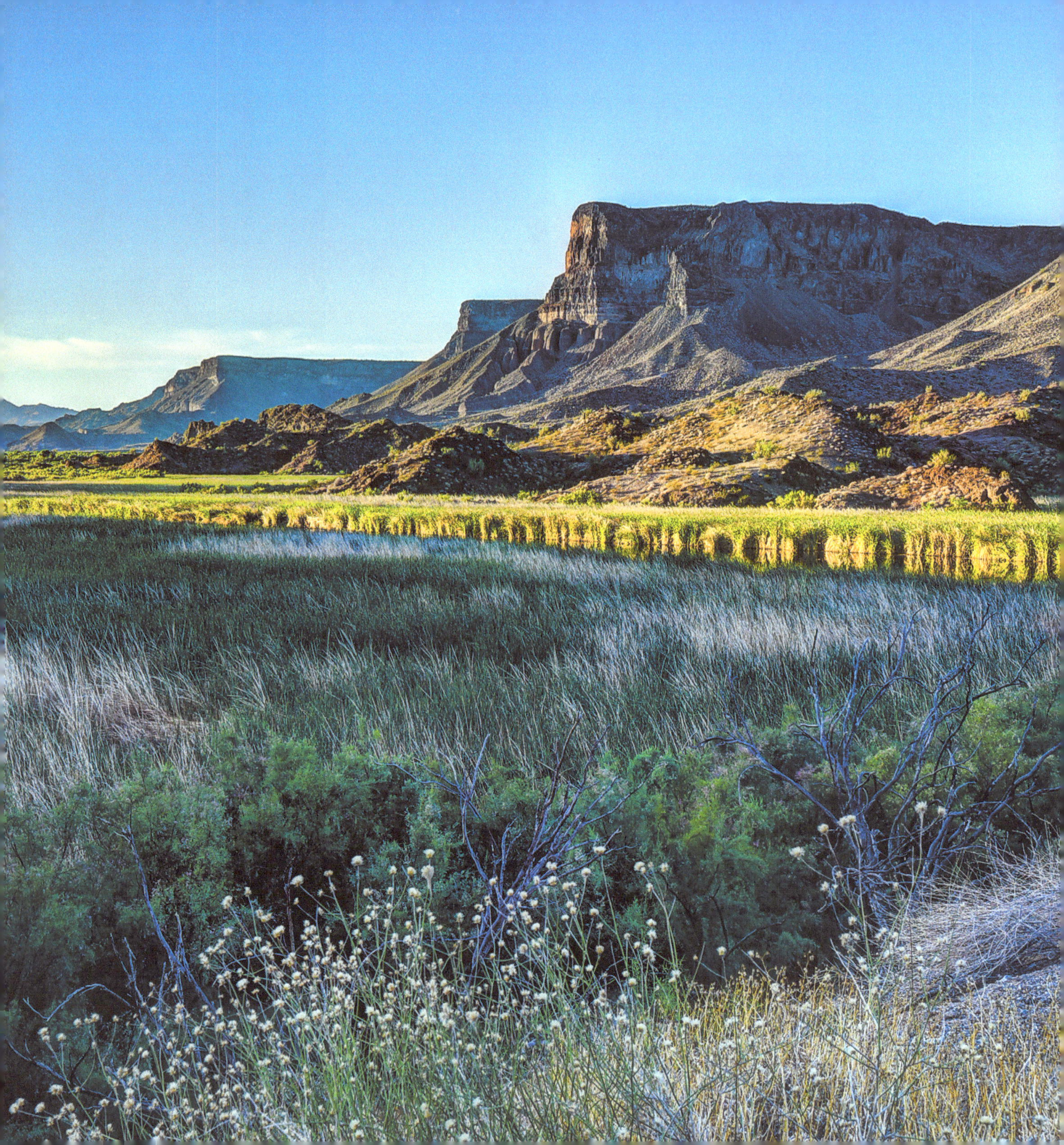

PURPOSE
REFLECTIONS

You Live With His Purpose

And we know that God causes all things to work together for good to those who love God, to those who are called according to His purpose.
Romans 8:28

When you come to Christ and are saved, you enjoy a new life filled with purpose, His purpose. He has a plan for your life. With the Holy Spirit leading, you can run in the direction of His will, and accomplish all that He gives you to do each day. His high calling for your life includes being conformed to the image of Christ (Romans 8:29), accomplishing all the good works He has planned for you (Ephesians 2:10), and bringing Him great glory that He may be glorified and supreme over all things (1 Corinthians 15:28). You can smile even in difficult times knowing He is causing all things to work together for good.

Lord, thank You for giving me new and abundant life filled with Your purpose and plan. I want to live out all You have in mind for me and bring You great glory. In Jesus' Name, Amen.

For those whom He foreknew, He also predestined to become conformed to the image of His Son.

Romans 8:29

See that you humble yourselves, and take no place before God or man but that of a servant. That is your work; let that be your one purpose and prayer. God is faithful. Just as water seeks and fills the lowest place, so the moment God finds the creature empty, His glory and power flow in to exalt and to bless. He that humbles himself—that must be our one aim—shall be exalted; that is God's aim. By His mighty power and in His great love He will do it.

Humility: The Beauty of Holiness — Andrew Murray

So, what is our duty now as believers saved by grace? Our primary purpose is to know Jesus Christ personally with ever-deepening intimacy (Phil. 3:8–11). If we read Scripture, pray, meditate, journal, or fast, let us do it for the sole purpose of knowing His mind. If we worship, serve, partake of communion, or spend time in the company of believers, let us learn about Him through His transforming work in others. If we feed the poor, defend the weak, comfort the lonely, or proclaim the gospel to a broken and needy world, let our walking in His sandals give us firsthand knowledge of His character. Let every trial or triumph bring us closer to knowing Christ's nature and to understanding His purposes.

Insights on Romans — Chuck Swindoll

He has saved us and called us with a holy calling, not according to our works, but according to his own purpose and grace, which was given to us in Christ Jesus before time began.

2 Timothy 1:9 csb

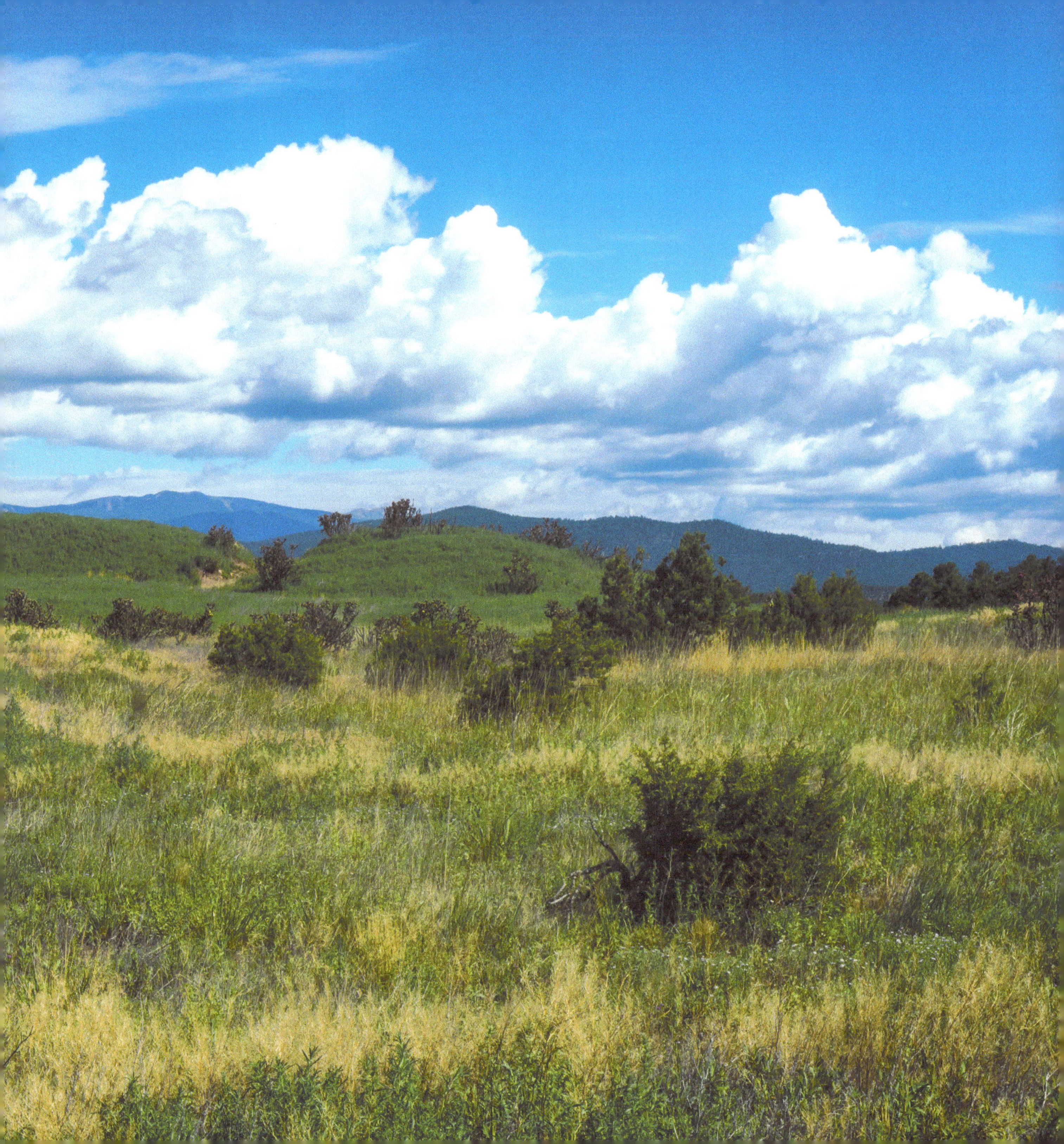

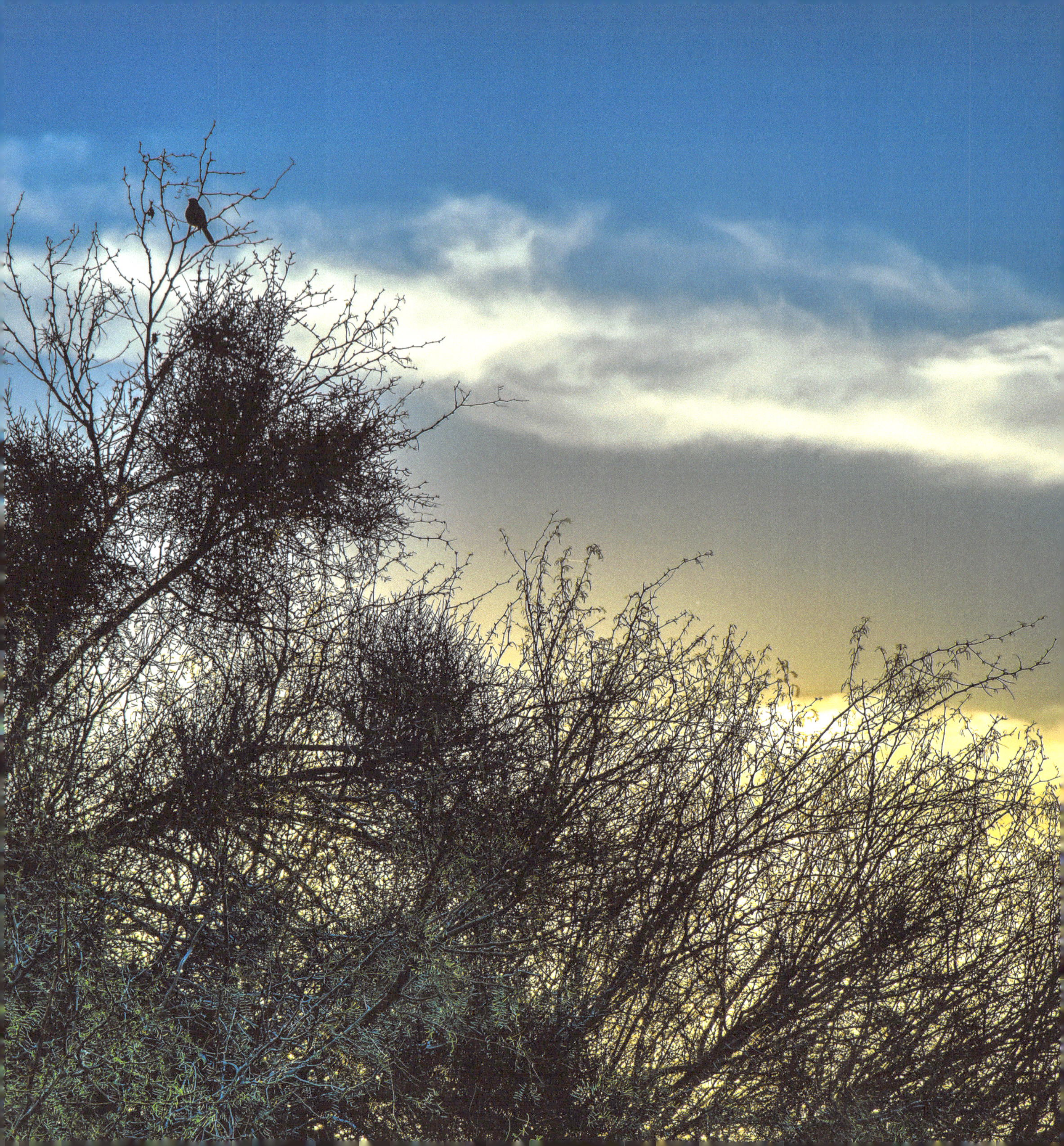

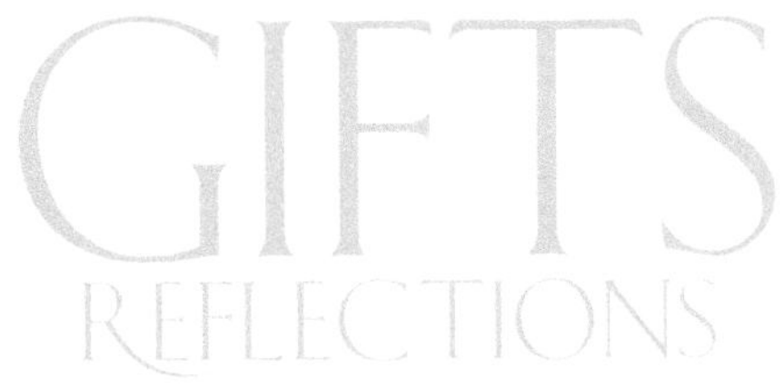

YOU HAVE SPIRITUAL GIFTS

Since we have gifts that differ according to the grace given to us,
each of us is to exercise them accordingly.
ROMANS 12:6

The power of the gospel is seen not only in saving us but also sanctifying us as we grow spiritually, and then carries us into His plan and purpose as we surrender to Him and serve Him using our gifts given by the Spirit. You are gifted by the Holy Spirit to serve the Lord and the church is the best place to exercise your gifts. In the church—the body of Christ—people come to know Christ, know and love God's Word, grow in their relationship with the Lord, use their Holy Spirit-given gifts for God's glory, and minister to one another with Christ's love, care, and concern in the power of the Holy Spirit.

Lord, thank You for giving me spiritual gifts according to Your grace. Help me exercise my gifts in the power of the Holy Spirit. In Jesus' Name, Amen.

Now there are varieties of gifts, but the same Spirit.

1 Corinthians 12:4

The Church is an organism rather than an organization, and this figure of the body with its several members is a definite reminder of the place and limits of each individual Christian.

Romans: A Devotional Commentary, XII-XVI — W.H. Griffith Thomas

You may say that you are not important. But you are! That part next to you is more important, perhaps, but he cannot go on without you and he is dependent upon you, and he will suffer if you are not in a fit condition to do your part. So all of us are vital, all of us are essential, all of us have a great privilege, and the way to avoid problems and disasters is always to be thinking of the whole body and especially of the Head. Then you will always be looking at Him, keeping your eye on Him, ready, sensitive, responsive, so that when He initiates an action, it is carried out. That is the great New Testament doctrine of the Christian church and her unity and functioning.

Romans: Christian Conduct, Exposition of Chapter 12 — D. Martyn Lloyd-Jones

The church's one foundation is Jesus Christ, her Lord;
she is His new creation, by water and the word.
From heav'n He came and sought her to be His holy bride;
with His own blood He bought her, and for her life He died.

Samuel John Stone

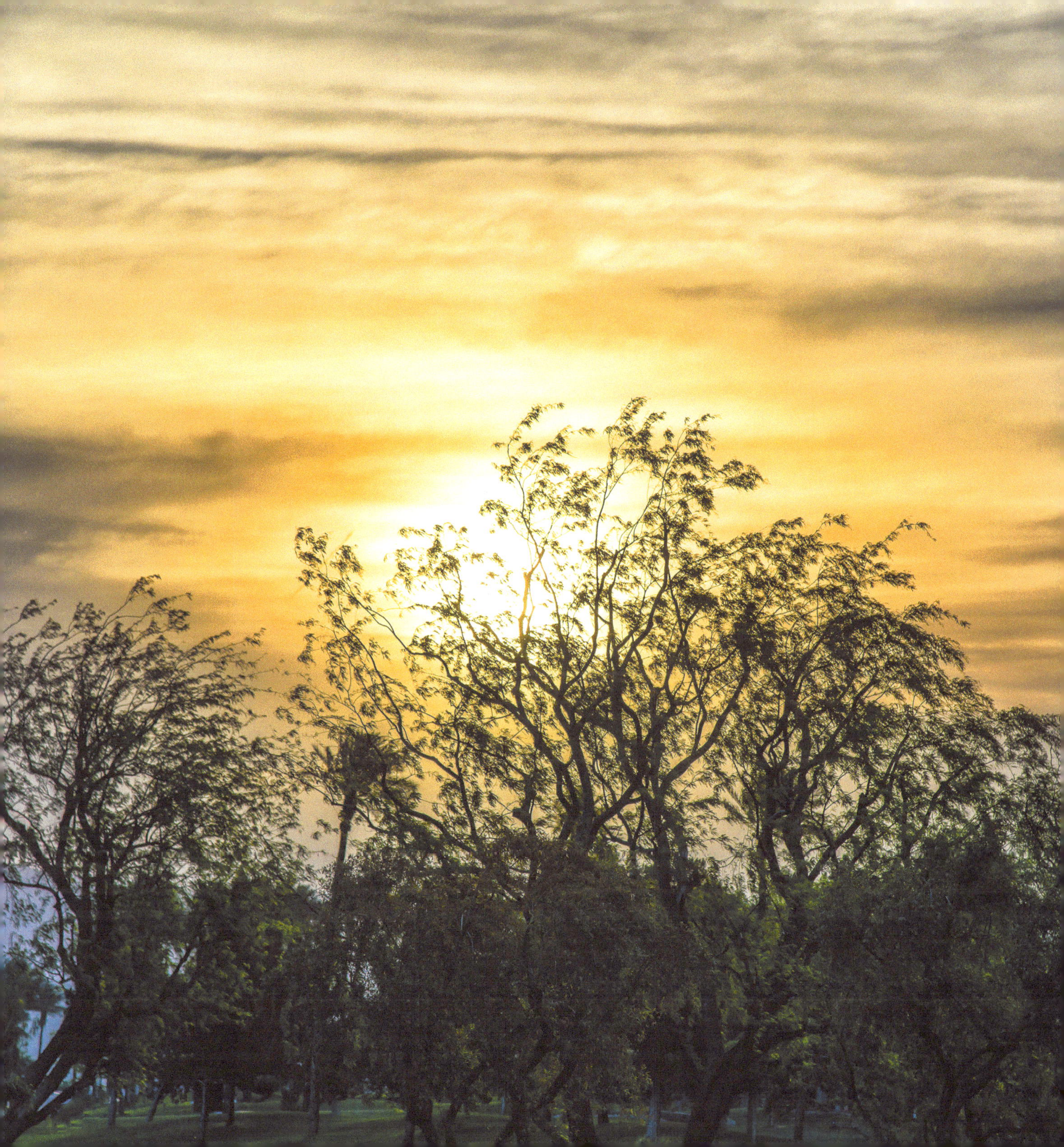

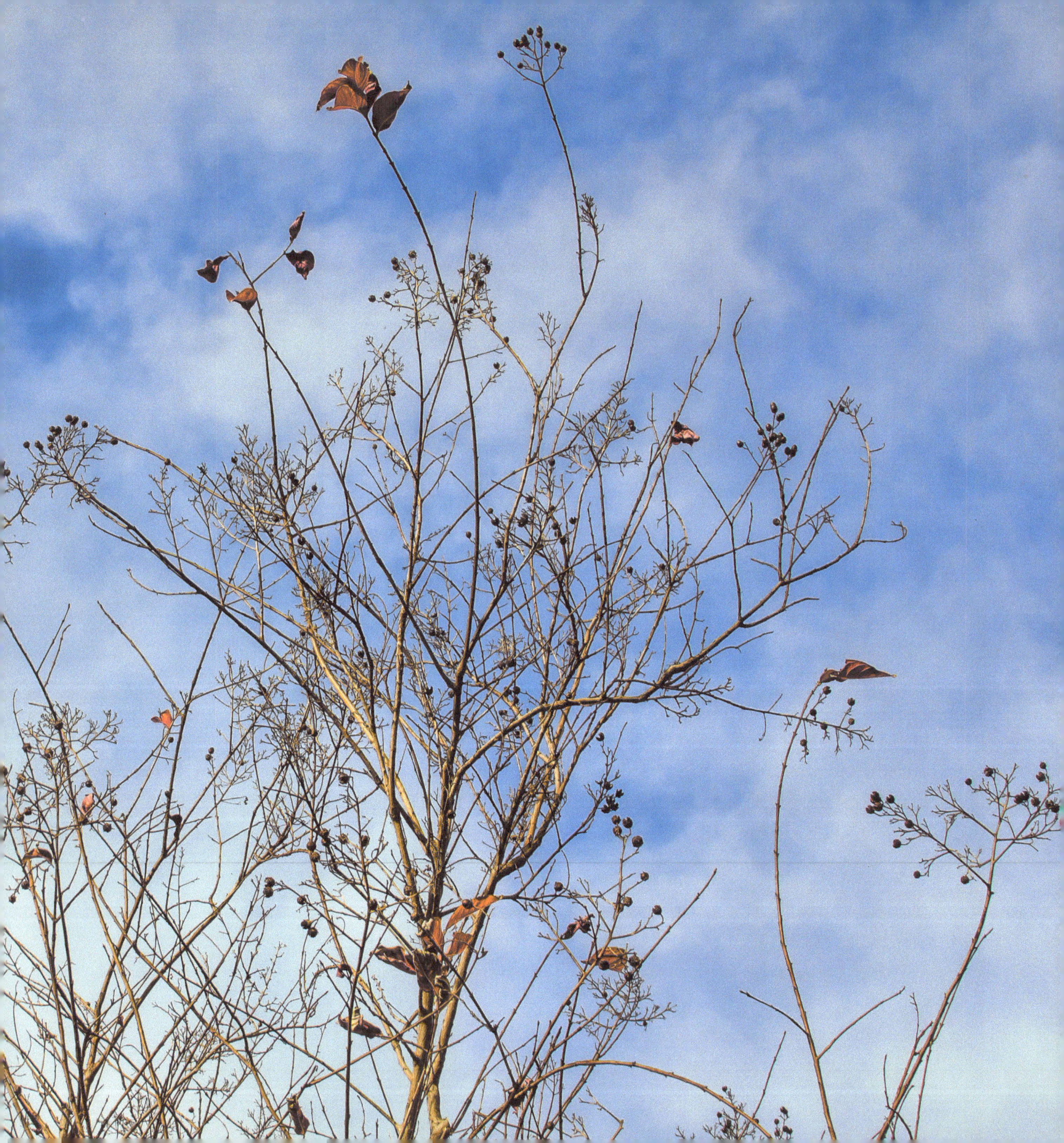

MINISTRY REFLECTIONS

You Have a Ministry

Be devoted to one another in brotherly love; give preference to one another in honor; not lagging behind in diligence, fervent in spirit, serving the Lord.
Romans 12:10-11

God has a ministry for you now that you know Him. Jesus Christ lives in you and wants to touch lives in and through you. You might think of ministry as "Jesus Christ in action." As you live with Christ during your brief stay on earth, you will see Him accomplish His work in and through you as you exercise your spiritual gifts in the power of the Holy Spirit. When you see a need in the church, the body of Christ, you can step out by faith and help meet that need. There is nothing so exciting as watching the Lord Jesus Christ at work as He ministers in and through you to touch a lost and hurting world.

Lord, thank You for giving me a ministry. Open my eyes to the needs around me. Live in and through me today to touch a lost and hurting world. In Jesus' Name, Amen.

And there are varieties of ministries, and the same Lord.

1 Corinthians 12:5

For we are God's masterpiece. He has created us anew in Christ Jesus, so we can do the good things he planned for us long ago..

Ephesians 2:10 nlt

I serve a risen Saviour, He's in the world today
I know that He is living, whatever men may say
I see His hand of mercy, I hear His voice of cheer
And just the time I need Him He's always near.

Refrain: He lives, He lives, Christ Jesus lives today
He walks with me and talks with me along life's narrow way
He lives, He lives, Salvation to impart
You ask me how I know He lives? He lives within my heart.

In all the world around me I see His loving care
And though my heart grows weary I never will despair
I know that He is leading, through all the stormy blast
The day of His appearing will come at last. *Refrain*

Rejoice, rejoice, O Christian Lift up your voice and sing
Eternal hallelujahs to Jesus Christ, the King
The Hope of all who seek Him, the Help of all who find
None other is so loving, so good and kind. *Refrain*

Alfred H. Ackley

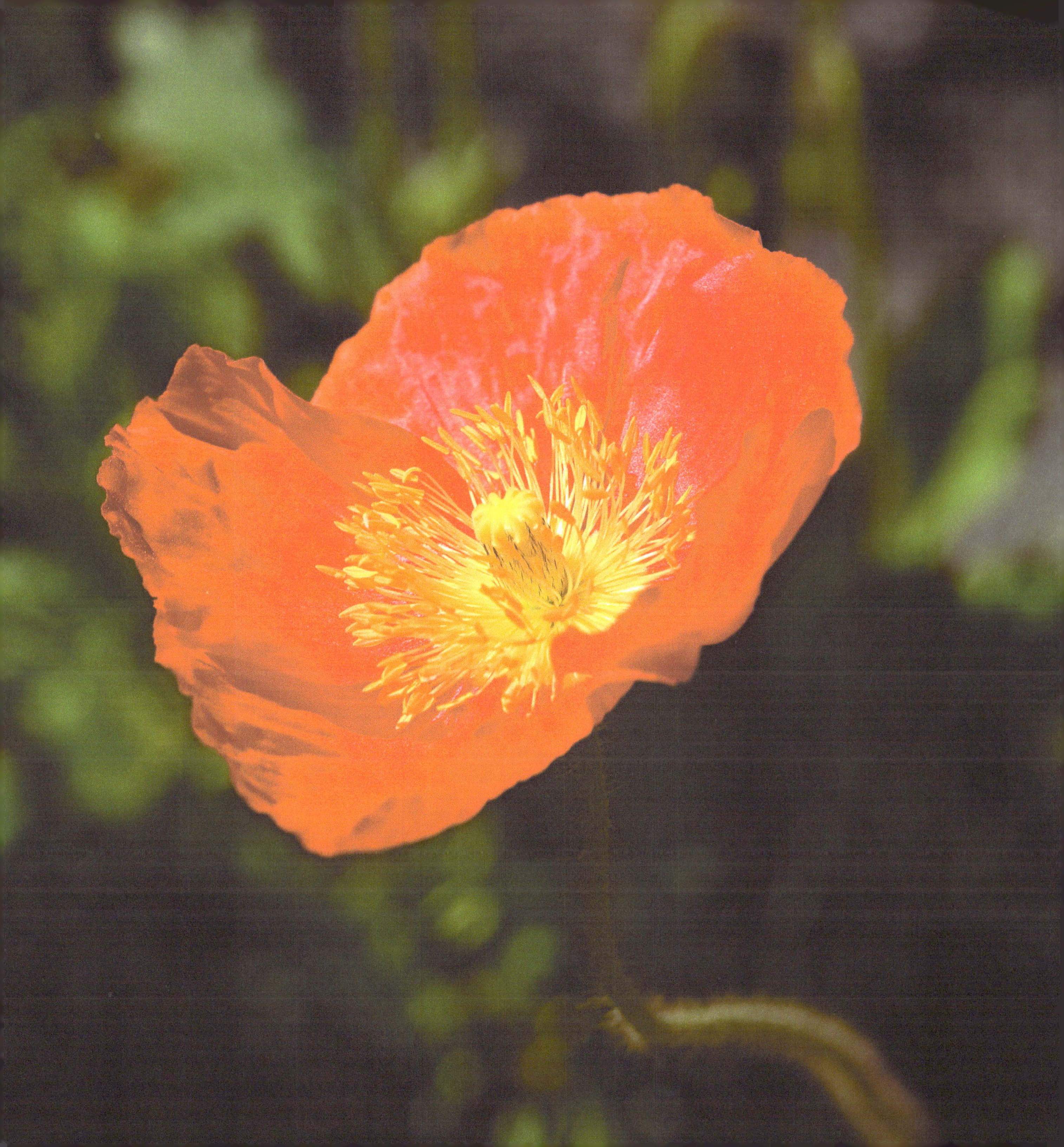

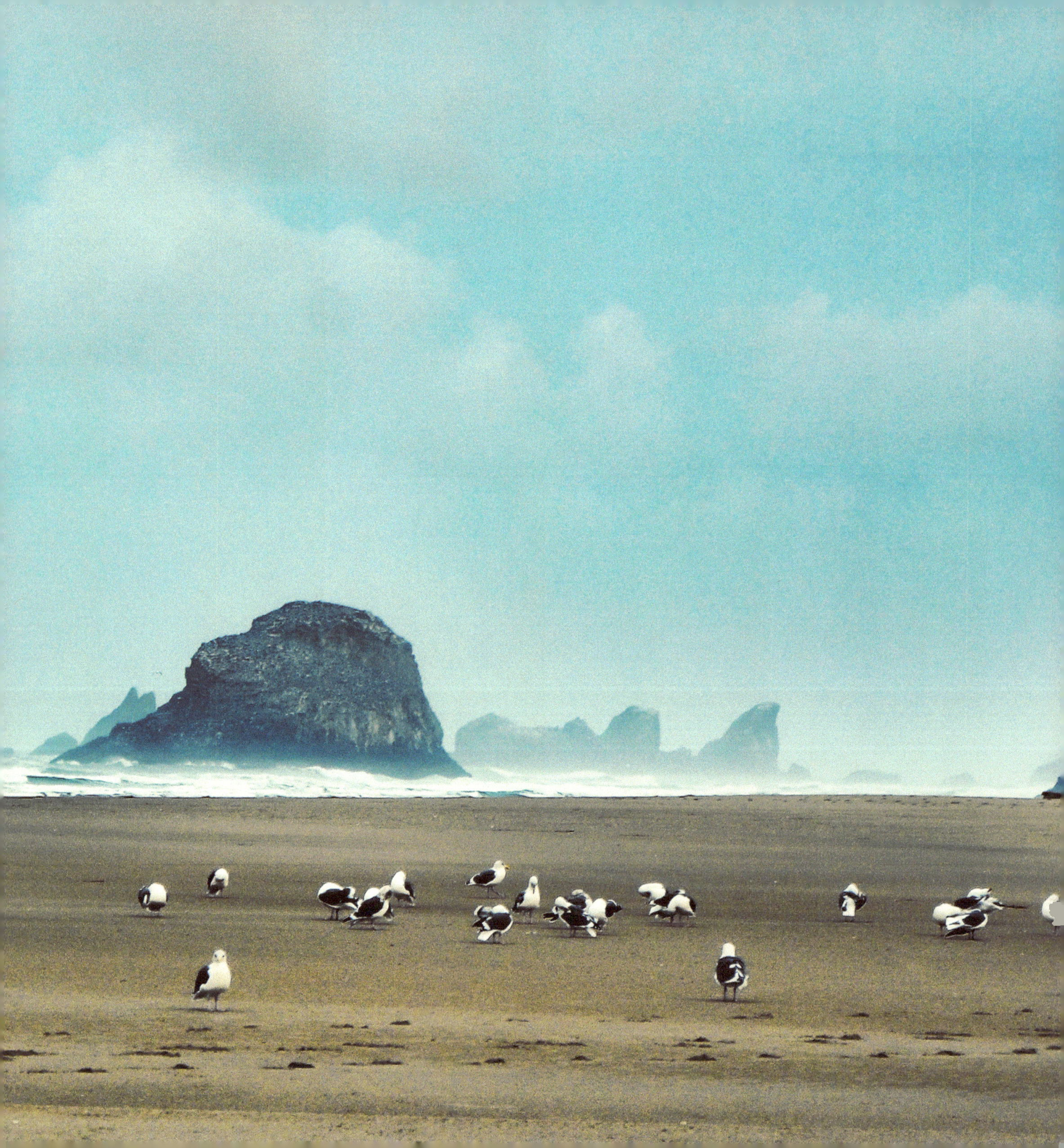

INFLUENCE
REFLECTIONS

You Influence Others

Love each other with genuine affection…When God's people are in need, be ready to help them…
Live in harmony with each other…Do all that you can to live in peace with everyone.
Romans 12:10,13,16,18

What happens when a person lives the life of God's righteousness? Lives are influenced by the Lord Jesus Christ as He lives in and through them. The life of God's righteousness shining in a person looks magnificently brighter and different than the darkness and desolation of the world. God has blessed us with relationships in what is called "the body of Christ" (1 Corinthians 12:27). Every day is your opportunity to influence those in relationship with you because of Christ. As you walk in love, day by day, God's love changes everything including you and those around you.

Lord, thank You for the relationships You have given me. Open my eyes to those around me and help me love them with Your unconditional love. In Jesus' Name, Amen.

Walk in love, just as Christ also loved you and gave Himself up for us, an offering and a sacrifice to God as a fragrant aroma.

Ephesians 5:2

Clothe yourselves with the Lord Jesus Christ.

Romans 13:14 niv

When I get up in the morning I put on my clothes, intending them to be part of me all day, to go where I go and do what I do. They cover me and make me presentable to others. That is the purpose of clothes. In the same way, the apostle is saying to us, "Put on Jesus Christ when you get up in the morning. Make Him a part of your life that day. Intend that He go with you everywhere you go, and that He act through you in everything you do. Call upon His resources. Live your life in Christ.

Ray Stedman

My one desire and prayer is that I may be filled with your love. I am bankrupt of love; I have not love enough of my own to love my neighbor as myself. Shed abroad your love in my heart through your Holy Spirit.

Daily Prayers — F.B. Meyer

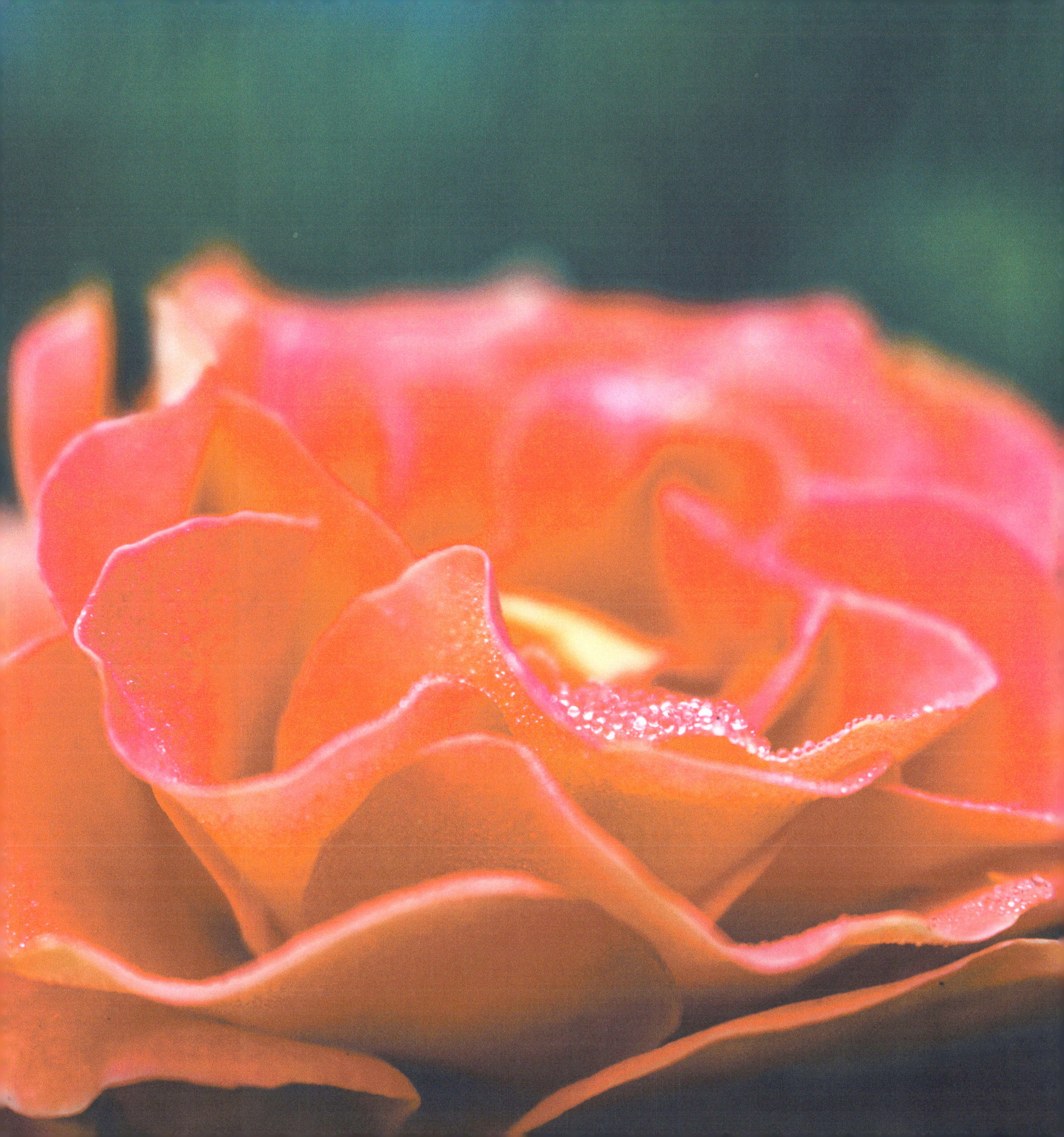

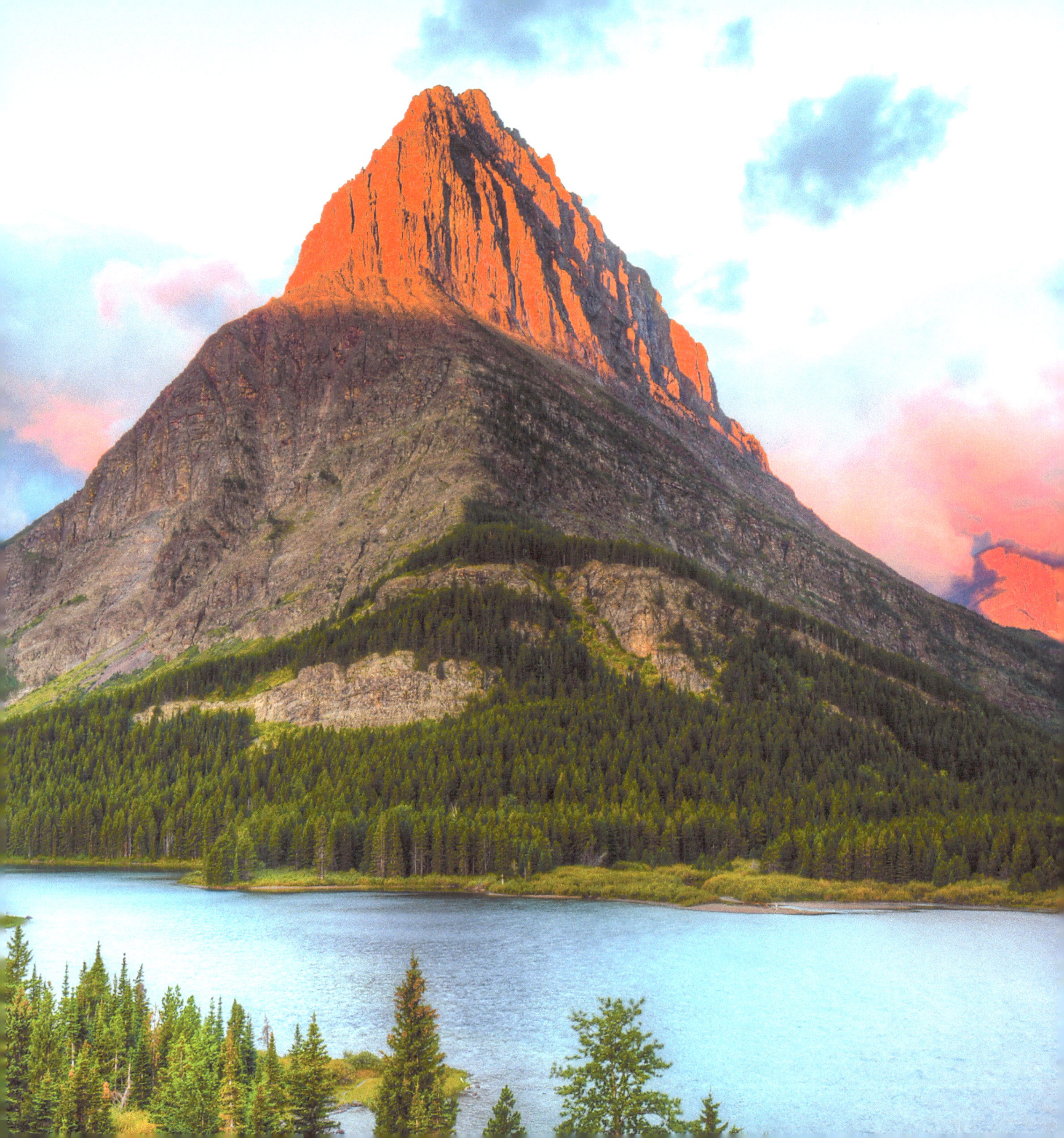

GLORIFICATION

REFLECTIONS

You Are Glorified in Christ

These whom He predestined, He also called; and these whom He called, He also justified; and these whom He justified, He also glorified.
Romans 8:30

Your salvation is finished from God's point of view. Note the past tense of all He has done for you—predestined, called, justified, and glorified. The work is finished and nothing can rob you of it. Oh, beloved, immerse yourself in the assurance and eternal security that God is revealing to you today. God knows you by name and loves you. He has made you complete in Christ and in Him you are honored, lifted up, and favored forever. Your glorified life now shows off the glorious splendor of God's presence, the compassionate kindness of His love, and the incomprehensible nature of His power as you glorify Him.

Lord, thank You for all You have done for me. May my life glorify You, and show off Your presence, love and power every day. In Jesus' Name, Amen.

Glorify the God and Father of our Lord Jesus Christ with a united mind and voice.

Romans 15:6 HCSB

Don't you know that your body is a sanctuary of the Holy Spirit who is in you, whom you have from God? You are not your own, for your were bought at a price. Therefore glorify God in your body.

1 Corinthians 6:19-20 HCSB

These verses introduce us to five great doctrines regarding believers in Jesus Christ: (1) foreknowledge, (2) predestination, (3) effectual calling, (4) justification, and (5) glorification. These five doctrines are so closely connected that they have rightly and accurately been described as "a golden chain of five links."

Romans — James Montgomery Boice

So we look forward, and are waiting and looking unto and hasting unto the coming of this blessed, glorious day of God, the day of glory, the day of our glorification, the day of our ultimate, final, full salvation.

Romans, Chapter 8:5-17, Sons of God — D. Martyn Lloyd-Jones

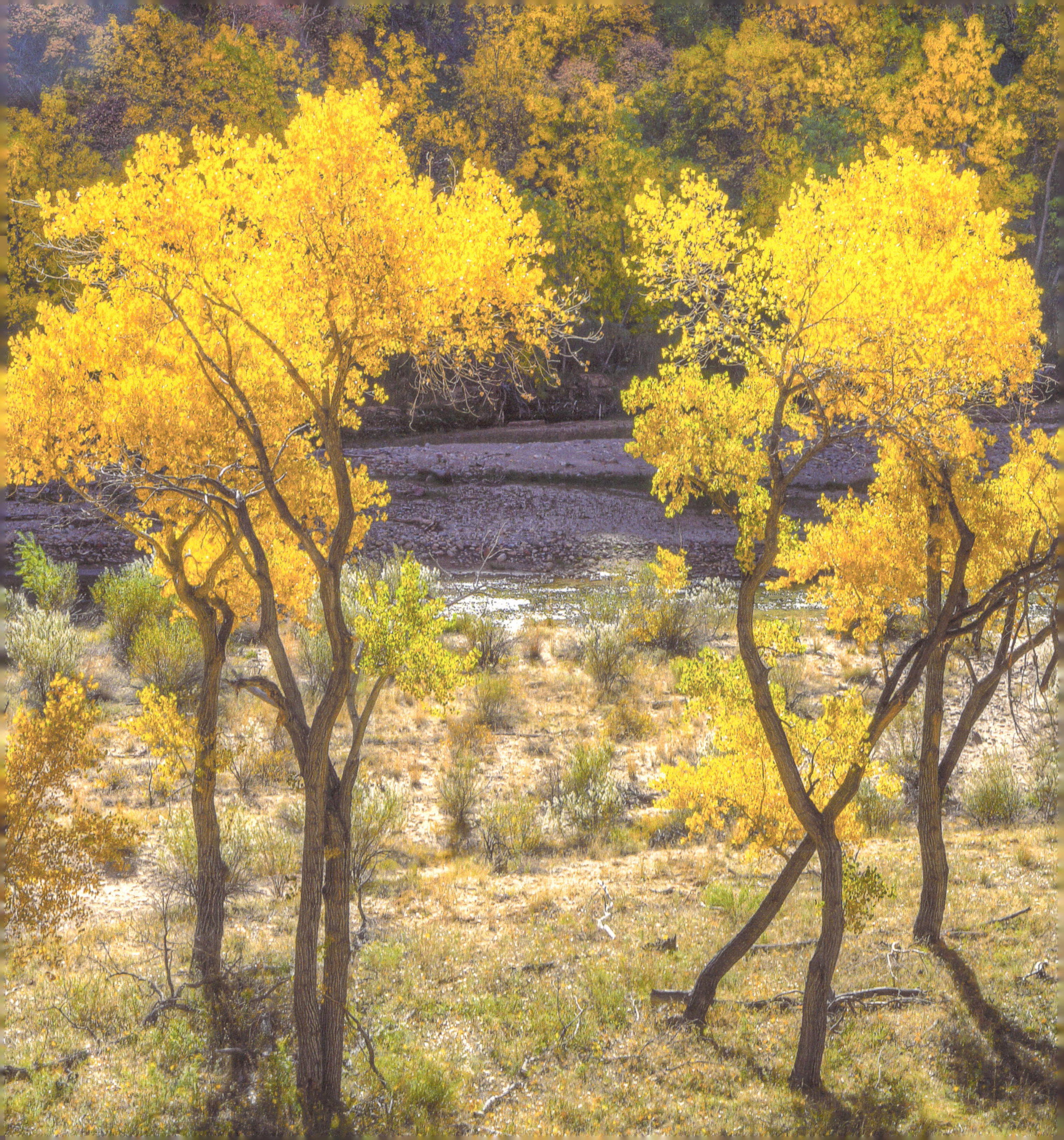

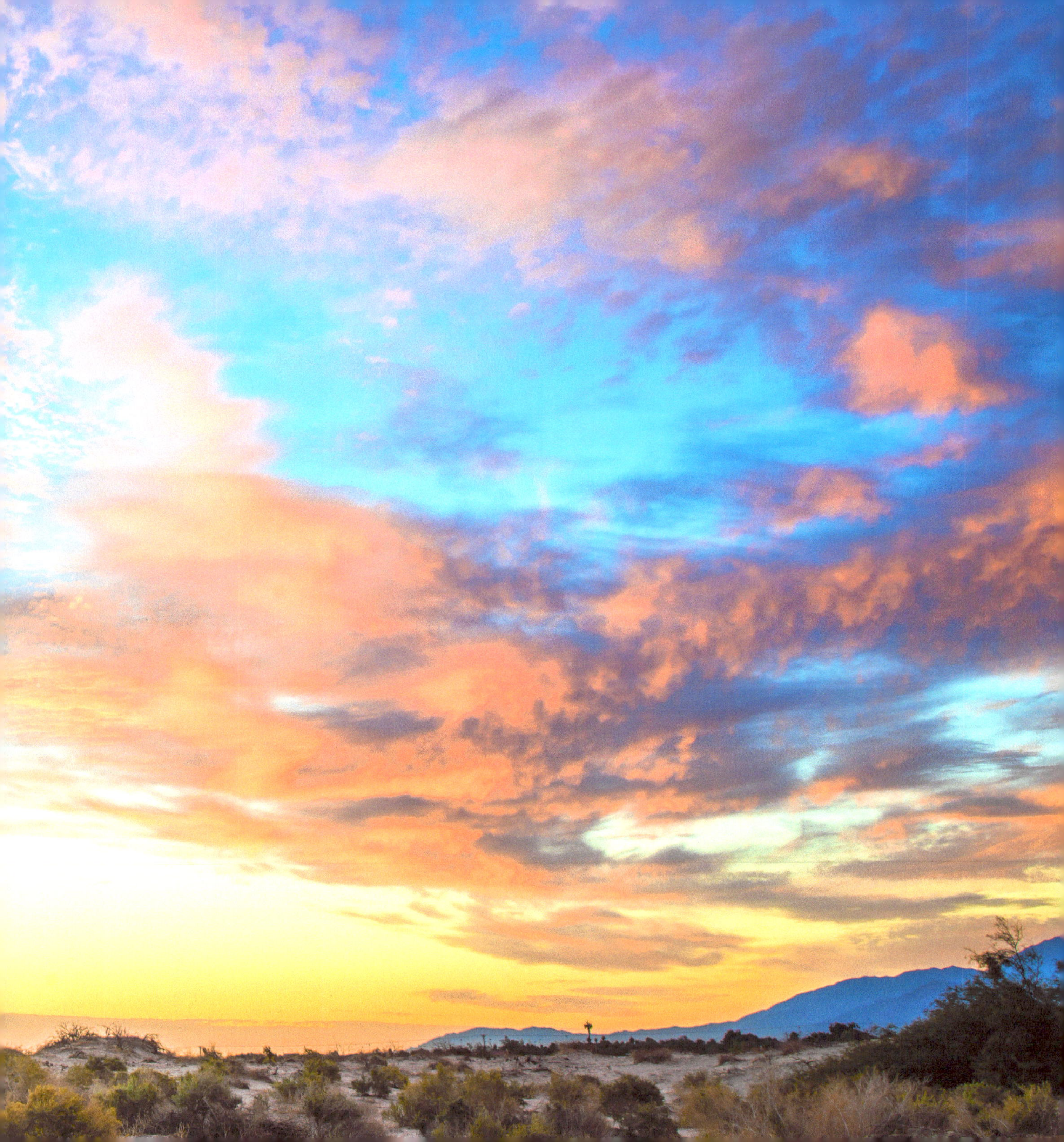

INHERITANCE

REFLECTIONS

You Are An Heir With Christ

The Spirit himself testifies with our spirit that we are God's children. Now if we are children, then we are heirs—heirs of God and co-heirs with Christ….

Romans 8:16-17 NIV

Your union with Christ gives you a whole new identity. You are a child of God. Because you are God's child, you are His heir and a fellow heir with Christ. The Holy Spirit is given to you now as a pledge of your inheritance (Ephesians 1:13-14). Your inheritance includes the kingdom of God, redemption, salvation, and is imperishable and eternal, is considered a reward, and is characterized by His glory (1 Corinthians 15:50, Ephesians 1:18, Colossians 3:24, Hebrews 1:14, 9:15). In Christ as a co-heir with Him, you are wealthy with the "riches of the glory of His inheritance in the saints" (Ephesians 1:18).

Lord, thank You for making me Your child and a co-heir with Christ. Help me remember how You have blessed me with an imperishable eternal inheritance. In Jesus' Name, Amen.

Blessed be the God and Father of our Lord Jesus Christ, who has blessed us with every spiritual blessing in the heavenly places in Christ, just as He chose us in Him before the foundation of the world, that we would be holy and blameless before Him. In love He predestined us to adoptions as sons through Jesus Christ to Himself, according to the kind intention of His will, to the praise of the glory of His grace, which He freely bestowed on us in the Beloved.

Ephesians 1:3-6

Do you live rejoicing day by day in the fact that you are a child of God, and because a child, then an heir? What is your heart set upon? At what are you looking? Is it only at this present life and world? Are you like the heroes of the faith in Hebrews 11? Are you like the patriarchs and the saints? Are you looking forward? Are you like the believers in the New Testament? They were all looking forward. We are only given "the earnest of our inheritance" here; the great inheritance itself is to come.

Romans, Chapter 8:5-17, Sons of God — D. Martyn Lloyd-Jones

The term "heir," clearly suggests something additional to and higher than sonship…It is for us to accept, to enter upon, and to enjoy this marvelous wealth of privilege. No wonder that the Apostle is so certain, in view of this great prospect, that we shall be saved and kept to the very end. This is how the Christian life will be completed.

Romans: A Devotional Commentary VI-XI — W.H. Griffith Thomas

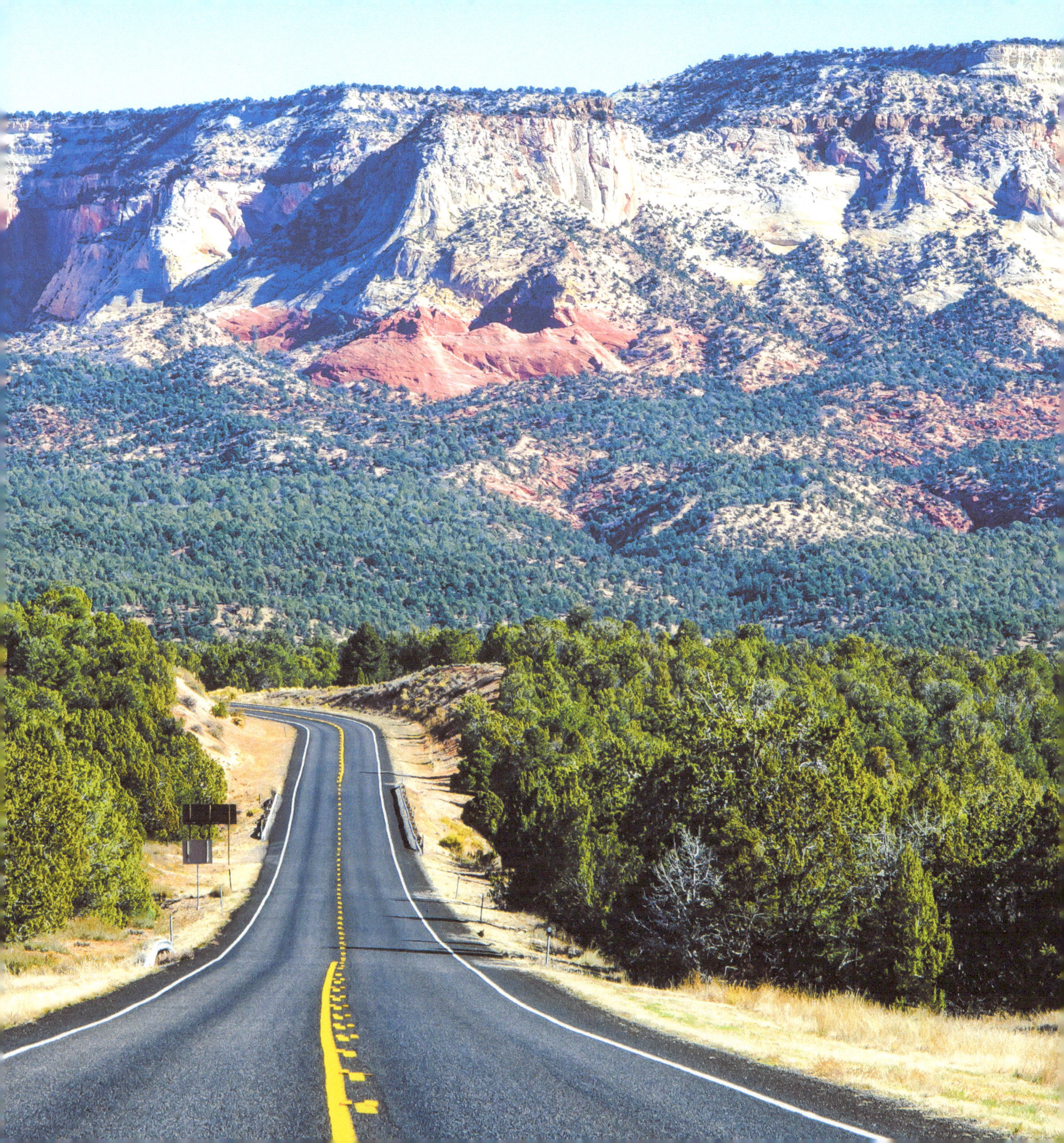

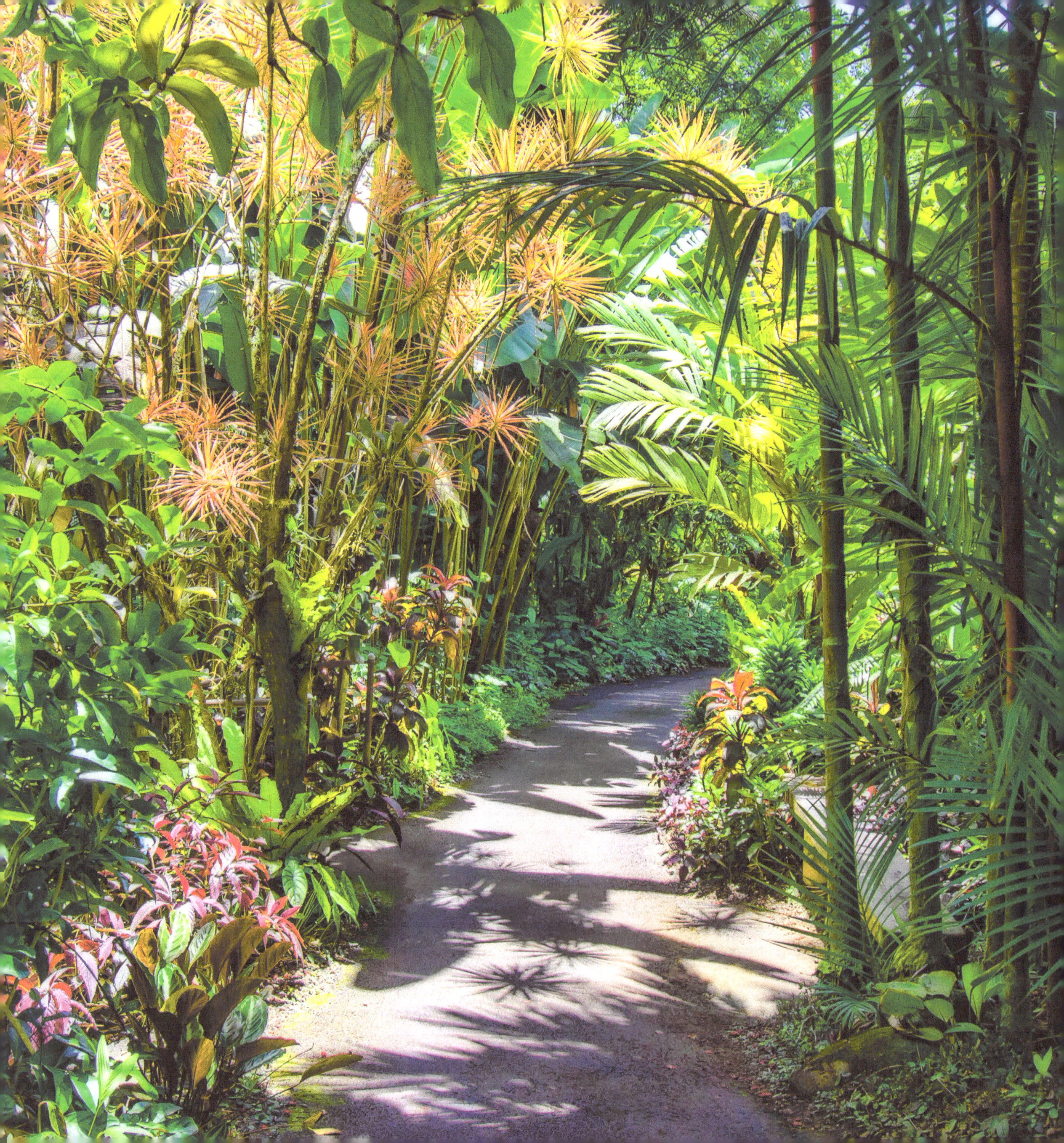

ETERNAL LIFE
REFLECTIONS

You Have Eternal Life in Christ

The gift of God is eternal life in Christ Jesus our Lord.
Romans 6:23 niv

The power of the gospel is seen in the realization of its promised hope—eternal life with Jesus Christ. The gospel contains everything you need to know to be saved, forgiven of your sins, and inherit eternal life (John 3:16, Titus 3:7). Jesus has completed everything so that you may be forgiven and inherit eternal life. He "canceled out the certificate of debt consisting of decrees against us, which was hostile to us; and He has taken it out of the way, having nailed it to the cross" (Colossians 2:14). You have a future and a hope that nothing and no one can touch. Heaven is your home, God's kingdom is your realm, and life with Christ is forever.

Lord, thank You for giving me the gift of eternal life in Christ. I look forward to my home with You in heaven, enjoying Your kingdom, and living with Christ forever. In Jesus' Name, Amen.

No eye has seen, no ear has heard, and no mind has imagined
what God has prepared for those who love Him.

1 Corinthians 2:9 nlt

Now you are a pilgrim on earth, a servant of the Lord, and as the Bride making herself ready for her Bridegroom, you are on your way home where you will live with the Lord forever. Here we see hope in the now and the not yet in life. Someday we shall step into heaven and our faith will become sight. "For now we see in a mirror dimly, but then face to face; now I know in part, but then I will know fully just as I also have been fully known" (1 Corinthians 13:12). John tells us "Beloved, now we are children of God, and it has not appeared as yet what we will be. We know that when He appears, we will be like Him, because we will see Him just as He is" (1 John 3:2).

The Proof of God's Amazing Love — Catherine Martin

Always remember that you are never alone. The Lord Jesus Christ is with you and promises to "never leave you nor forsake you" (Hebrews 13:5 esv). S.D. Gordon puts it this way: "Jesus never sends a man ahead alone. He blazes a clear way through every thicket and woods, and then softly calls, 'Follow me. Let's go on together, you and I.' He has been everywhere that we are called to go. His feet have trodden down smooth a path through every experience that comes to us. He knows each road, and knows it well: the valley road of disappointment with its dark shadows; the steep path of temptation down through the rocky ravines and slippery gullies; the narrow path of pain, with the brambly thornbushes so close on each side, with their slash and sting; the dizzy road along the heights of victory; the old beaten road of commonplace daily routine. Everyday paths He has trodden and glorified, and will walk anew with each of us. The only safe way to travel is with Him alongside and in control."

The Proof of God's Amazing Love — Catherine Martin

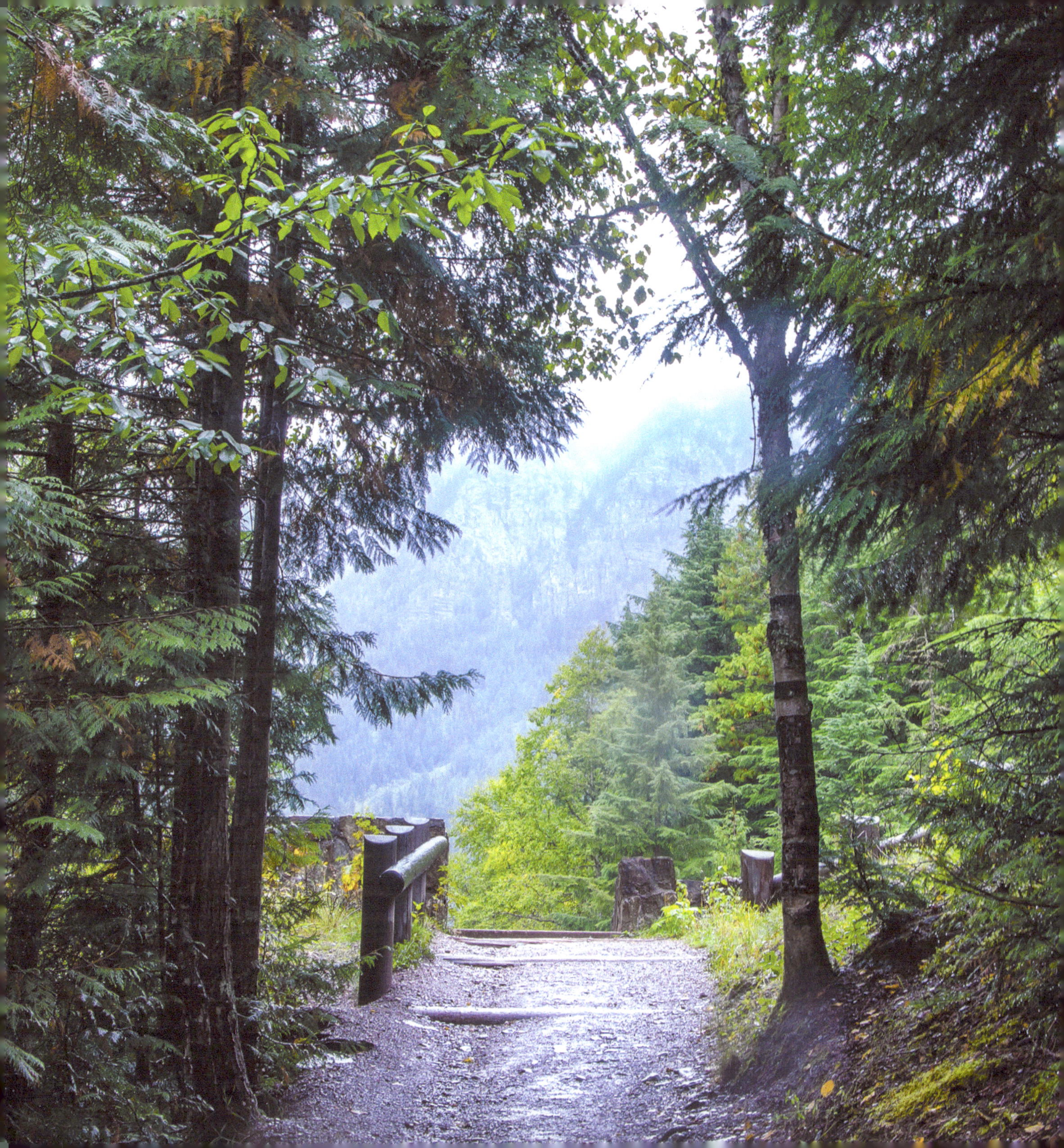

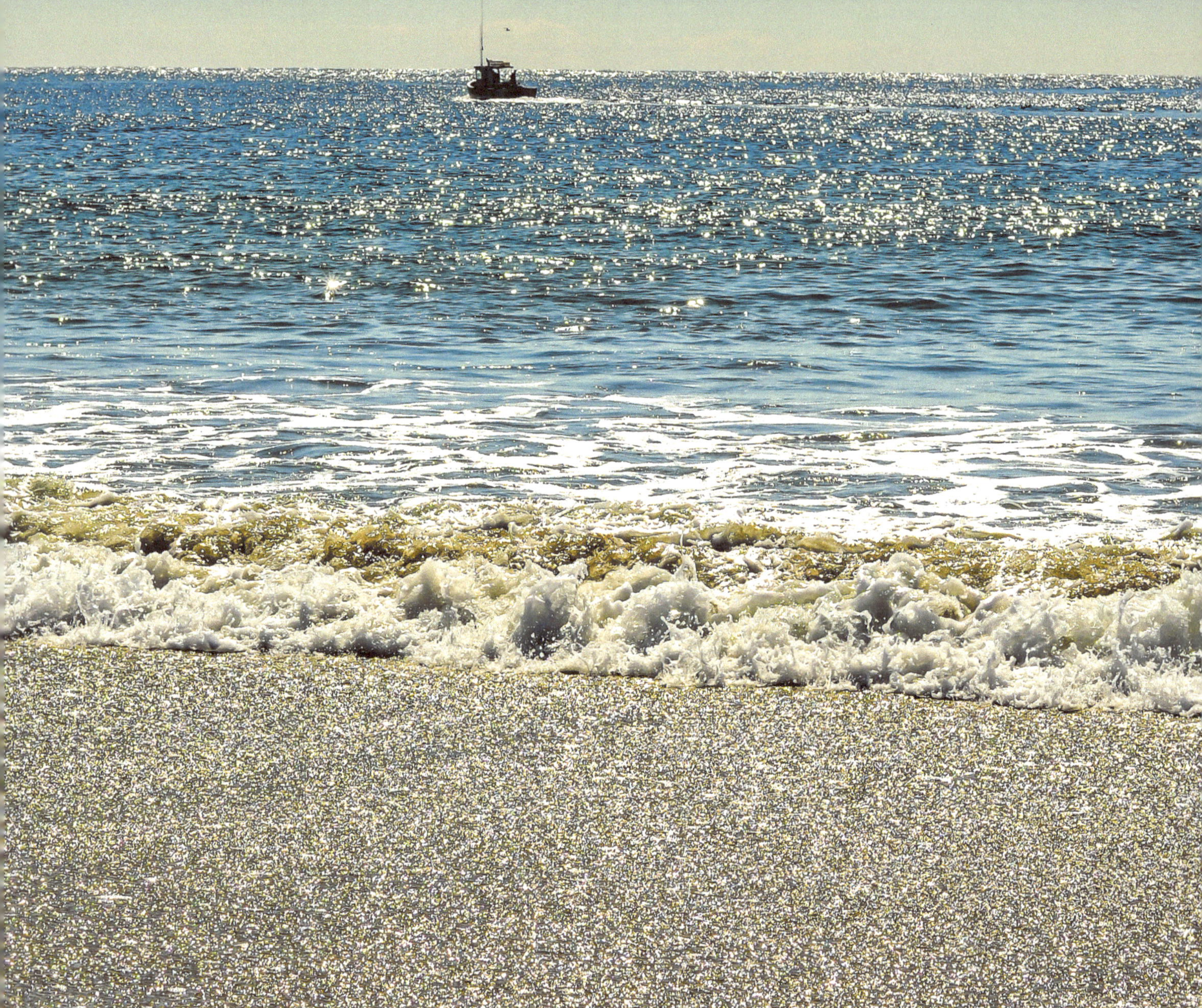

HOW TO BECOME A CHRISTIAN

Do you realize that God loves you and has a plan for your life? Have you entered into a love relationship with Him by asking Jesus into your life? Jesus Christ is God's only provision for man's sin. Through Him, you can know God's love and plan for your life. Jesus said, "Behold, I stand at the door and knock; if anyone hears My voice and opens the door, I will come in to him and will dine with him, and he with me" (Revelation 3:20). We must individually receive Jesus Christ to know God's love and experience His plan for our lives. We see in John 1:12 that "as many as received Him, to them He gave the right to become children of God, even to those who believe in His name." You can receive Jesus right now by praying a simple prayer something like this, "Lord Jesus, I need You. Thank You for dying on the cross for me. I ask You now to come into my life, forgive my sins, give me eternal life, and make me the person You want me to be. In Jesus' name, Amen. "

If you prayed that prayer for the first time, I am thrilled with your decision as I believe it is the most important choice you will make in life. When I made the decision to trust Christ as my Savior, I discovered life-changing truths that will encourage you in your relationship with Him. You have had the opportunity to discover these truths in *The Power of the Gospel*, but I will summarize them here so you can be encouraged in your new life in Christ.

As a result of your decision *you are given a new life*. How can that be? First, all your sins are forgiven by God (past, present, and future sins). In the Bible, God says if you confess your sins, He is faithful and just to forgive your sins and cleanse you from all unrighteousness (I John 1:9). Confession means "agreeing with God" about any sin in your life. You never have to be afraid to come to God to confess your sin. In fact, it has been said that God never cleansed any of our excuses, only sin. Jesus died on the cross to pay the penalty for your sin. On the basis of what Jesus has done, we are able to ask God to forgive us and cleanse us from all unrighteousness.

God also cleanses you from all unrighteousness so that you may now have a love relationship with Him. This love relationship is possible because *Jesus now makes His home in your heart.* He is always with you and will never leave you. Nothing can separate you from Him and nothing can change His great love for you. That's important to remember, especially during the trials of life. You can talk to Him anytime and anywhere. He always hears your prayers. He may answer your prayers differently than you expect, but He always has your best interests in mind. He is at work in you, making you the person you are meant to be (Philippians l:6).

Finally, one of the greatest gifts God gives you is *eternal life*. For God so loved the world that He gave His one and only Son, that whoever believes in Him shall not perish but have eternal life (John 3:l6). You have a future that extends far beyond this life. And you have a place in heaven being prepared for you by Jesus Himself (John 14:2).

How can you begin growing in your new relationship with Christ? Several ways. You are embarking on the greatest adventure of your life—knowing God. First, *choose a good Bible.* The Bible is God's Word — it contains everything God wants you to know about Himself, His ways, His desires, your own life, and His goals for you. Part of the adventure occurs as you discover God in His Word. Choose a good translation of the Bible like *The New King James Version*, *The New American Standard Bible*, *The New International Version*, or *The New Living Translation*. If you desire to choose a Study Bible, the very best are *The Life Application Bible*, *The NIV Study Bible*, or *The International Inductive Study Bible*. You will be able to find a good Bible at any Christian bookstore or online at christianbook.com. Reading and studying God's Word is a most important part of your life with God, so choosing a good Bible is an important investment in your new relationship with the Lord.

Establish a quiet time each day to read the Bible and talk with God. Intimacy in your relationship with God takes time. Choose a place conducive to thought and reflection. God desires an intimate, ongoing relationship with you. Draw near to Him and talk to Him about everything. For more resources, information, and encouragement for your quiet time, check out Quiet Time Ministries at www.quiettime.org. This website is power packed with Feature Article devotional posts, Speaking Ministry information, myPhotoWalk Devotional Photography publications, and extensive quiet time books, studies, audio, and video Resources in our Online Store.

I encourage you to *attend a good church on Sundays* to worship God, meet other Christians, and learn from the Bible, God's Word. I also encourage you to join a good Bible study to continue growing in your relationship with the Lord. I lead an online Bible study on Thursday mornings—you can find out more at Quiet Time Ministries at https://quiettime.org/online-bible-studies.html.

Oh, how He loves you dear friend. His love is the love that reached out to Paul on the Damascus road, the love that held him strong even when his circumstances were seemingly impossible as he preached the gospel, and it is the love that will never let you go. "For God so loved the world, that He gave His only begotten Son, that whoever believes in Him shall not perish, but have eternal life" (John 3:16).

May you always remember you have a future and a hope in Jesus and you can look forward to being with Him forever for you have received the gift of eternal life. Until that day when you step into heaven may you "grow in the grace and knowledge of our Lord and Savior Jesus Christ. To Him be the glory, both now and to the day of eternity. Amen" (2 Peter 3:18).

God bless you.

In His Love and Service,
Catherine

THE ROMANS ROAD TO SALVATION

One of the most well-known summaries of the gospel is called "The Romans Road to Salvation." These powerful truths from Romans lay out the heart of the gospel—our need for the gospel, God's provision, how we may experience forgiveness of sins and eternal life, and the results. In these verses you see what is on the heart of God and His plan and purpose for you. You might want to look at each of the verses in your Bible for thought and reflection. For deeper study in the book of Romans, I encourage you to get the Quiet Time Experience, *The Proof of God's Amazing Love—Embrace the Power of the Gospel of Christ.*

- We all need salvation because we have all sinned: "For all have sinned and fall short of the glory of God" (Romans 3:23).
- The penalty for sin is death: "For the wages of sin is death, but the free gift of God is eternal life in Christ Jesus our Lord" (Romans 6:23).
- Jesus Christ died for our sins; He paid the price that we might be forgiven: "But God demonstrates His own love toward us, in that while we were yet sinners, Christ died for us" (Romans 5:8).
- We receive salvation and eternal life through Jesus Christ: "If you confess with your mouth Jesus as Lord, and believe in your heart that God raised Him from the dead, you will be saved; for with the heart a person believes, resulting in righteousness, and with the mouth he confesses, resulting in salvation…for whoever will call on he name of the Lord will be saved" (Romans 10:9-10,13).
- Salvation through Christ brings us into an eternal relationship with God: ""Therefore, having been justified by faith, we have peace with God through Lord Jesus Christ" (Romans 5:1). "Therefore, there is now no condemnation for those who are in Christ Jesus" (Romans 8:1).

APPENDIX

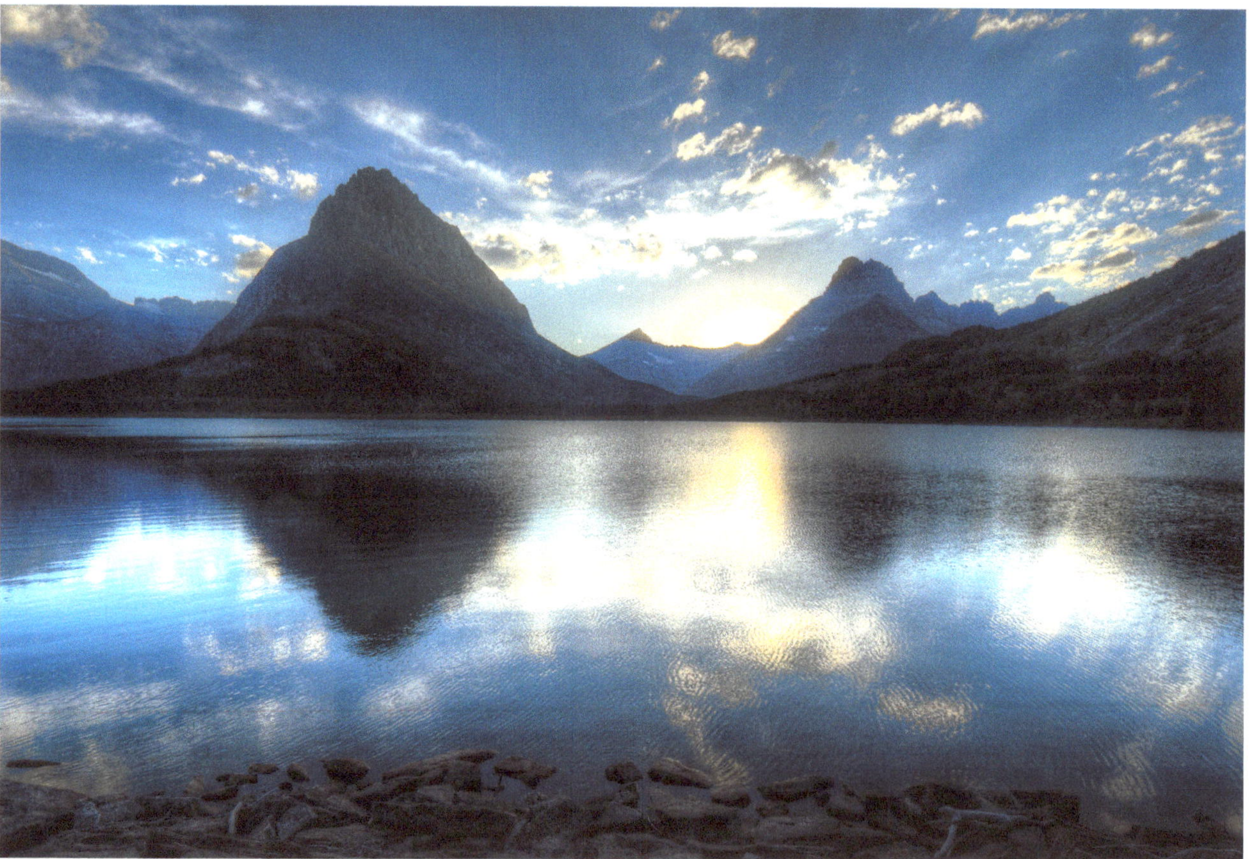

PHOTOGRAPHY

COVER

Cover and Interior Photography by Catherine Martin, myPhotoWalk—SmugMug, catherinemartin.smugmug.com, Custom Prints and Inspirational Gifts.

The Power of the Gospel, 2017, Newport Beach, California, USA, Nikon D810, Micro-Nikkor 200mm, FL 200mm, ISO 200, f/11, 1/100sec.

THE POWER OF THE GOSPEL

THE CATHERINE MARTIN SMUGMUG GALLERIES — Catherine Martin's very favorite images expressing themes from *myPhotoWalk* chosen from photoshoots at Glacier National Park, Antelope Canyon, Hawaii, Tuscany, Sedona, Klamath Falls, Newport Beach, San Francisco, Los Angeles, Hollywood, Beverly Hills, Laguna Beach, Santa Monica, San Diego, and La Jolla, as well as the Mojave-Sonoran Desert. Enjoy.

Page 15: A Heart Overflowing, 2015, Oak Creek, Sedona, Arizona, USA, Nikon D800E, Nikkor 24-120mm, FL 105mm, ISO 100, f/22, 0.4sec.

Page 16, The Sedona Sunflower, 2021, Slide Rock State Park, Sedona, Arizona, USA, Sony A6000, Zeiss 16-70mm, FL 26mm, ISO 100, f/11, 1/160sec.

Page 19: A Firm Foundation, 2012, Monument Valley Navajo Tribal Park, Olijato-Monument Valley, Utah, USA, Nikon D7000, Nikkor 18-105mm, FL 105mm, ISO 160, f/11, AEB.

Page 20: The Gift Of Grace, 2012, Hawaii Tropical Botanical Garden, Papaikou, Island of Hawaii, Hawaii, USA, Nikon D7000, Nikkor 50mm, FL 50mm, ISO 160, f/16, 1/1600sec.

Page 23: Footsteps In The Sea, 2012, Pauoa Bay, Waimea, Island of Hawaii, Hawaii, USA, Nikon D7000, Nikkor 18-105mm, FL 66mm, ISO 100, f/5.6, 1/500sec.

Page 24: Jesus, Your Prayer Partner, 2015, El Santuario de Chimayo, Chimayo, New Mexico, USA, Sony A6000, 16-70 Zeiss, FL 16mm, ISO 125, f/4, 1/160sec.

Page 27: The Way Of The Cross, 2015, El Santuario de Chimayo, Chimayo, New Mexico, USA, Sony A6000, Zeiss 16-70mm, FL 16mm, ISO 100, f/11, 1/125sec.

Page 28: Reeds By The Water, 2013, Coachella Valley Preserve, Palm Desert, California, USA, Nikon D7000, Nikkor 18-105mm, FL 50mm, ISO 100, f/5, 1/160sec.

Page 31: His Love Sets Me Free, 2014, Mountain Vista Lake, Palm Desert, California, USA, Nikon D800E, 24-120mm, FL 100mm, ISO 100, f/6.3, 1/160sec.

Page 32: Looking To The Lord, 2016, Corona Del Mar State Beach, Corona Del Mar, Newport Beach, California, USA, Nikon D810, Nikkor 80-400mm, FL 175mm, ISO 1600, f/11, 1/5000sec.

Page 35: Flower In The Garden, 2021, Newport Beach, California, USA, Sony A6000, Zeiss 16-70mm, FL 36mm, ISO 100, f/6.3, 1/200sec.

Page 36: Knowing Christ, 2013, Lake McDonald, Glacier National Park, Montana, USA, Nikon D7000, 12-24mm, FL 24mm, ISO 100, f/11, AEB.

Page 39: Every Good Thing, 2013, Many Glacier, Glacier National Park, Montana, USA, Nikon D7000, 12-24mm, FL 16mm, ISO 100, f/11, 1/4sec.

Page 40: Mercy, 2012, Lower Antelope Slot Canyon, Antelope Canyon Navajo Tribal Park, Page, Arizona, USA, Nikon D7000, 18-105mm, FL 18mm, ISO 125, f/13, AEB.

Page 43: High Places, 2012, Mittens West East Merrick Buttes, Monument Valley Navajo Tribal Park, Olijato-Monument Valley, Utah, USA, Nikon D7000, 18-105mm, FL 18mm, ISO 200, f/11, AEB.

Page 44: Always Hope, 2015, Oak Creek Canyon, Sedona, Arizona, USA, Nikon D800E, Nikkor 24-120mm, FL 38mm, ISO 1000, f/11, 1/25sec.

Page 47: Hope In Rivers Of Difficulty, 2013, West Fork Trail, Sedona, Arizona, USA, Nikon D7000, 12-24mm, FL 22mm, ISO 100, f/11, AEB.

Page 48: God's Spirit Resting On You, 2012, Pauoa Bay, Waimea, Island of Hawaii, Hawaii, USA, Nikon D7000, Nikkor 12-24mm, FL 12mm, ISO 200, f/7, 1/200sec.

Page 51: He Strengthens Me, 2016, Corona Del Mar State Beach, Corona Del Mar, Newport Beach, California, USA, Nikon D810, Nikkor 80-400mm, FL 370mm, ISO 100, f/8, 1/160sec.

Page 52: His Light For Your Path, 2013, Many Glacier, Glacier National Park, Montana, USA, Nikon D7000, Nikkor 12-24mm, FL 12mm, ISO 100, f/11, AEB.

Page 55: The Light Of The World, 2013, Many Glacier, Glacier National Park, Montana, USA, Nikon D7000, 18-105mm, FL 105mm, ISO 100, f/11, 1/100sec.

Page 56: Peace In Prayer, 2015, Valles Caldera National Preserve, Jemez Springs, New Mexico, USA, Sony A6000, Zeiss 16-70mm, FL 16mm, ISO 100, f/11, 1/200sec.

Page 59: The Power Of Love, 2012, Akaka Falls, Akaka Falls State Park, Honomu, Island of Hawaii, Hawaii, USA, Nikon D7000, 12-24mm, FL 12mm, ISO 160, f/10, 1/100sec.

Page 60: Waiting, 2015, Valles Caldera National Preserve, Jemez Springs, New Mexico, USA, Sony A6000, Zeiss 16-70mm, FL 70mm, ISO 100, f/6.3, 1/200sec.

Page 63: Ready To Fly, 2015, Osher Rainforest, California Academy of Sciences, Golden Gate Park, San Francisco, California, USA, Nikon D810, 70-300mm, FL 300mm, ISO 800, f/5.6, 1/2500sec.

Page 64: Watching And Waiting, 2015, Osher Rainforest, California Academy of Sciences, Golden Gate Park, San Francisco, California, USA, Nikon D810, Nikkor 70-300mm, FL 170mm, ISO 1250, f/5.6, 1/500sec.

Page 67: Loving One Another, 2013, Coachella Valley National Wildlife Refuge, Palm Desert, California, USA, Nikon D7000, Nikkor 70-300mm, FL 300mm, ISO 200, f/11, 1/400sec.

Page 68: A Quiet Place For Prayer, 2011, Cannon Beach Ecola State Park, Cannon Beach, Oregon, USA, Nikon D7000, 18-105mm, FL 26mm, ISO 250, f/6.3, 1/50sec.

Page 71: Surrender To God And His Word, 2011, Haystack Rock, Cannon Beach Haystack Hill State Park, Cannon Beach, Oregon, USA, Nikon D7000, 18-105mm, FL 92mm, ISO 400, f/5.6, 1/80sec.

Page 72: Beautiful Like A Butterfly, 2015, Osher Rainforest, California Academy Of Sciences, Golden Gate Park, San Francisco, California, USA, Nikon D810, 70-300mm, FL 300mm, ISO 1000, f/5.6, 1/500sec.

Page 75:The Majesty Of God, 2014. Indian Wells, California, USA, Nikon D800E, Nikkor 80-400mm, FL 320mm, ISO 1250, f/5.6, 1/800sec.

Page 76: Going Up To God, 2012, Dixie National Forest, Bryce Canyon National Park, Bryce Canyon, Utah, USA, Nikon D7000, Nikkor 18-105mm, FL 34mm, ISO 125, f/11, 1/8sec.

Page 79: The Glory Of Grace, 2012, The Virgin River, Zion National Park, Utah, USA, Nikon D7000, 18-105mm, FL 35mm, ISO 160, f/11, AEB.

Page 80: Journey, 2012 Pauoa Bay, Waimea, Island of Hawaii, Hawaii, USA, Nikon D7000, 18-105mm, FL 105mm, ISO 160, f/11, 1/125sec.

Page 83: Watching Always I Trust, 2011, San Gimignano, Siena, Tuscany, Italy, Nikon D7000, 18-105mm, FL 48mm, ISO 250, f/6.3, 1/320sec.

Page 84: Set Free, 2016, Corona Del Mar State Beach, Corona Del Mar, Newport Beach, California, USA, Nikon D810, Nikkor 80-400mm, FL 390mm, ISO 100, f/5.6, 1/400sec.

Page 87: Flying Above Saguaro, 2014, Lake Pleasant Regional Park, Morristown, Arizona, USA, Nikon D7000, Nikkor 80-400mm, FL 280, ISO 800, f/8, 1/2500sec.

Page 88: When God Revives, 2015, Hagiwara Tea Gardens, DeYoung Museum, Golden Gate Park, San Francisco, California, USA, Nikon D810, Nikkor 24-120mm, FL 78mm, ISO 400, f/8, 1/800sec.

Page 91: Drinking In His Everlasting Love, 2015, Wildlife World Zoo, Litchfield Park, Arizona, USA, Nikon D800E, 80-400mm, FL 260mm, ISO 400, f/6.3, 1/1250sec.

Page 92: The Open Door To Forgiveness, 2015, El Santuario de Chimayo, Chimayo, New Mexico, USA, Sony A6000, Zeiss 16-70mm, FL 29mm, ISO 100, f/9, 1/100sec.

Page 95: Flowers By The Sea, 2011, Corona Del Mar State Beach, Corona Del Mar, Newport Beach, California, USA, Nikon D7000, 18-105mm, FL 105mm, ISO 100, f/5.6, 1/320sec.

Page 96: Discovering The Way Of Salvation, 2015, Muir Woods National Monument, Mill Valley, California, USA, Nikon D810, 24-120mm, FL 24mm, ISO 100, f/16, AEB.

Page 99: The Open Gate, 2011, Principe Corsini Villa Le Corti, Val Di Pesa, Florence, Tuscany, Italy, Nikon D7000, Nikkor 18-105mm, FL 52mm, ISO 250, f/7.1, 1/400sec.

Page 100: Grace And Peace, 2015, Palace of Fine Arts, Marina District, San Francisco, California, USA, Nikon D810, 24-120mm, FL 65mm, ISO 400, f/7.2, 1/800sec.

Page 103: Loved By Jesus, 2015, Wildlife World Zoo, Litchfield Park, Arizona, USA, Nikon D800E, 80-400mm, FL 400mm, ISO 100, f/5.6, 1/320sec.

Page 104: Morning Song, 2014, Golden Pebble Habitat, Palm Desert, California, USA, Nikon D7000, Nikkor 80-400mm, FL 400mm, ISO 2000, f/5.6, 1/160sec.

Page 107: Chariot In The Clouds, 2013, Lake Havasu City, Arizona, USA, Nikon D7000, Nikkor 12-24mm, FL 24mm, ISO 100, f/11, AEB.

Page 108: Paradise, 2015, Muir Woods National Monument, Mill Valley, California, USA, Nikon D810, Nikkor 24-120mm, FL 24mm, ISO 125, f/22, AEB.

Page 111: In The Fiery Trial, 2008, Coronado Bridge, San Diego Bay, Coronado Island, San Diego, California, USA, Canon SD1100, 6.2-18.6mm, 18.6mm, ISO 80, f/4.9, 1/1000sec.

Page 112: The Valley Of Tears, 2013, Bill Williams River National Wildlife Refuge, Lake Havasu City, Arizona, USA, Nikon D7000, Nikkor 12-24mm, FL 24mm, ISO 100, f/11, AEB.

Page 115: No Worries, 2015, Pecos National Historical Park, Pecos, New Mexico, USA, Sony A6000, Zeiss 16-70mm, FL 38mm, ISO 100, f/16, 1/125sec.

Page 116: The Story Of Your Life, 2015, Coachella Valley Preserve, Palm Desert, California, USA, Nikon D800E, Nikkor 24-120mm, FL 120mm, ISO 100, f/11, AEB.

Page 119: Believing God For The Impossible, 2014, Coachella Valley Preserve, Palm Desert, California, USA, Nikon D800E, Nikkor 24-120mm, FL 100mm, ISO 100, f/5.6, 1/1250sec.

Page 120: Choosing The Best, 2015, Coachella Valley Preserve, Palm Desert, California, USA, Nikon D7000, Nikkor 35mm, FL 35mm, ISO 100, f/9, 1/100sec.

Page 123: Looking Up To God, 2019, Newport Beach, California, USA, Fujifilm X-T2, Fujinon XF18-55mm F2.8-4 R LM OIS, FL 20.5mm, ISO 100, f/11, 1/100sec.

Page 124: Revival In Difficult Times, 2011, Bird Rocks Yeon Natural Site, Cannon Beach Ecola State Park, Cannon Beach, Oregon, USA, Nikon D7000, 18-105mm, FL 80mm, ISO 250, f/6.3, 1/25sec.

Page 127: No More Tears, 2016, The Rose Garden, Newport Beach, California, USA, Nikon D810, Lensbaby Velvet 56, FL 56mm, ISO 400, f/5.6, 1/250sec.

Page 128: The Glory Of God, 2013, Many Glacier, Glacier National Park, Montana, USA, Nikon D7000, 12-24mm, FL 24mm, ISO 100, f/11, 0.6sec.

Page 131: All Joy And Peace, 2012, Zion National Park, Utah, USA, Nikon D7000, Nikkor 18-105mm, FL 52mm, ISO 160, f/11, AEB.

Page 132: In His Presence, 2014, Coachella Valley Preserve, Palm Desert, California, USA, Nikon D800E, Nikkor 24-120mm, FL 32mm, ISO 100, f/11, 1/8sec.

Page 135: The Steps Of The Godly, 2012, Zion National Park, Utah, USA, Nikon D7000, Nikkor 12-24mm, FL 12mm, ISO 160, f/13, 1/50sec.

Page 136: The Sweet Aroma Of Christ, 2012, Hawaii Tropical Botanical Garden, Papaikou, Island of Hawaii, Hawaii, USA, Nikon D7000, Nikkor 12-24mm, FL 18mm, ISO 250, f/7.1, 1/125sec.

Page 139: The City Of God, 2013, Going To The Sun Road, Glacier National Park, Montana, USA, Nikon D7000, Nikkor 18-105mm, FL 30mm, ISO 100, f/11, 0.6sec.

Page 140: Run Before The Wind, 2011, Corona Del Mar State Beach, Corona Del Mar, Newport Beach, California, USA, Nikon D7000, 50mm, FL 50mm, ISO 100, f/10, 1/400sec.

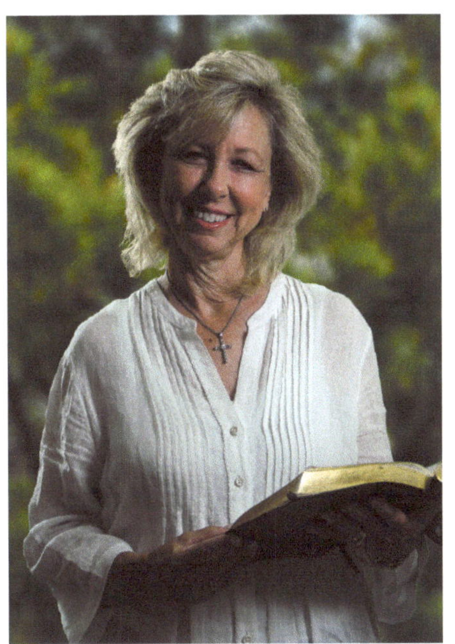

About the Author

Catherine Martin is a summa cum laude graduate of Bethel Theological Seminary with a Master of Arts degree in Theological Studies. She is founder and president of Quiet Time Ministries, a director of women's ministries for many years, and an adjunct faculty member of Biola University. She is the author of *Six Secrets to a Powerful Quiet Time, Knowing and Loving the Bible, Walking with the God Who Cares, Set my Heart on Fire, Trusting in the Names of God, Passionate Prayer,* and *Drawing Strength from the Names of God* published by Harvest House Publishers, and *Pilgrimage of the Heart, Revive My Heart* and *A Heart That Dances*, published by NavPress. She has also written *The Quiet Time Notebooks, Walk on Water Faith, One Holy Passion, The Proof of God's Amazing Love, A Heart on Fire, A Heart to See Forever, Run Before the Wind,* and *A Heart That Hopes in God*, published by Quiet Time Ministries Press. She is author of *Quiet Time Moments for Women* published by Christian Art Publishers. *myPhotoWalk Devotional Photography* publications include *Quiet Time Moments, Savoring God's Promises of Hope, The Story of Your Life,* and *A Day in the Life Of God.* As a popular keynote speaker at retreats and conferences, Catherine challenges others to seek God and love Him with all of their heart, soul, mind, and strength.

About Quiet Time Ministries

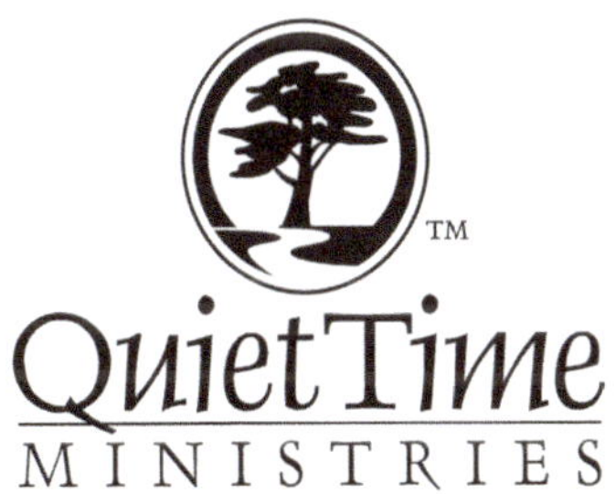

Quiet Time Ministries is a nonprofit religious organization under Section 501(c)(3) of the Internal Revenue Code. Cash donations are tax deductible as charitable contributions. We count on prayerful donors like you, partners with Quiet Time Ministries pursuing our goals of the furtherance of the Gospel of Jesus Christ and teaching devotion to God and His Word. Visit us online at www.quiettime.org to view special funding opportunities and current ministry projects. Your prayerful donations bring countless project to life!

Quiet Time Ministries | P.O. Box 14007 | Palm Desert, California 92255
1.800.925.6458 | catherine@quiettime.org | www.quiettime.org | www.myphotowalk.com

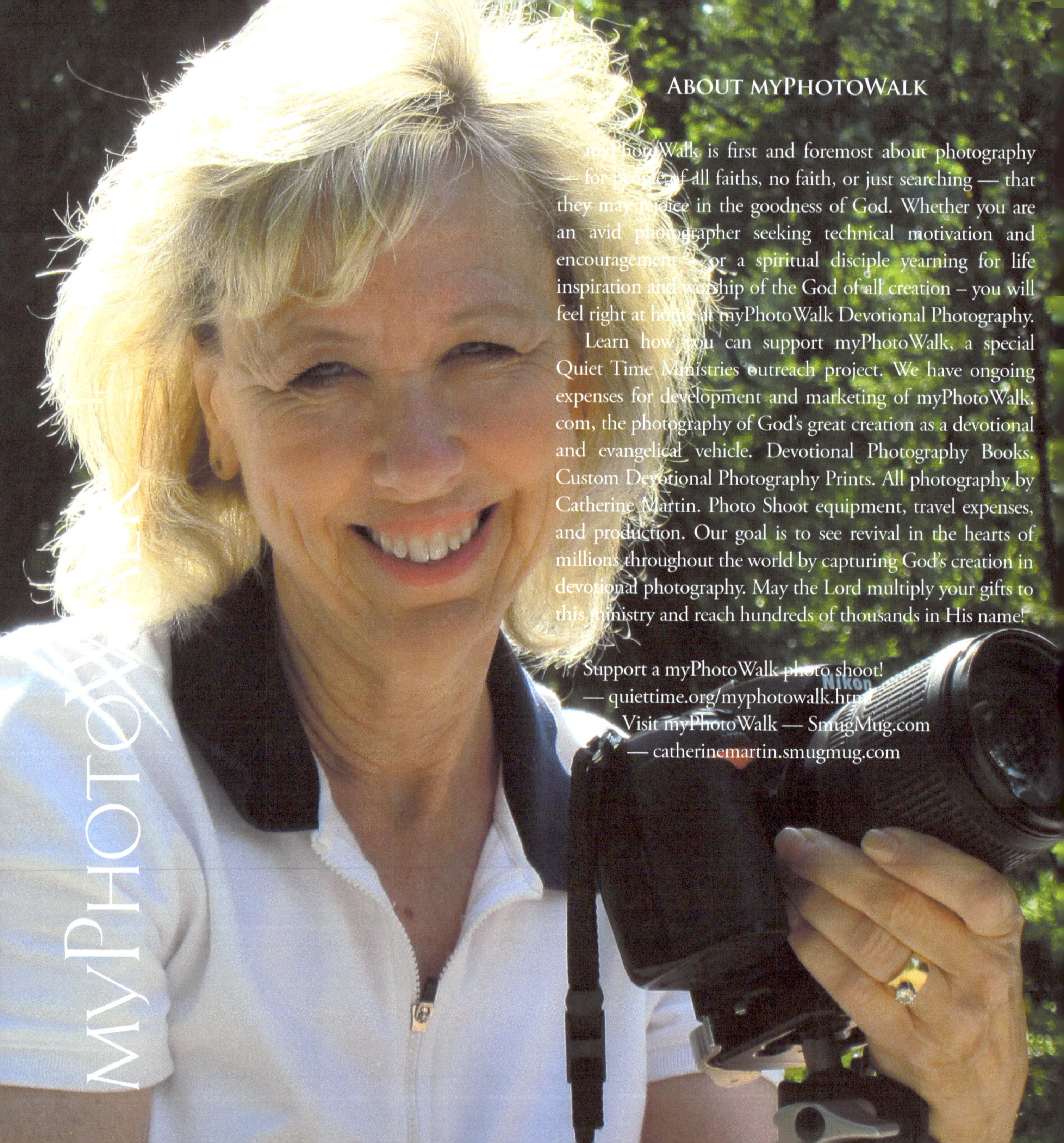

About myPhotoWalk

myPhotoWalk is first and foremost about photography — for people of all faiths, no faith, or just searching — that they may rejoice in the goodness of God. Whether you are an avid photographer seeking technical motivation and encouragement — or a spiritual disciple yearning for life inspiration and worship of the God of all creation – you will feel right at home at myPhotoWalk Devotional Photography.

Learn how you can support myPhotoWalk, a special Quiet Time Ministries outreach project. We have ongoing expenses for development and marketing of myPhotoWalk.com, the photography of God's great creation as a devotional and evangelical vehicle. Devotional Photography Books. Custom Devotional Photography Prints. All photography by Catherine Martin. Photo Shoot equipment, travel expenses, and production. Our goal is to see revival in the hearts of millions throughout the world by capturing God's creation in devotional photography. May the Lord multiply your gifts to this ministry and reach hundreds of thousands in His name!

Support a myPhotoWalk photo shoot!
— quiettime.org/myphotowalk.html
Visit myPhotoWalk — SmugMug.com
— catherinemartin.smugmug.com

myPhotoWalk

ACKNOWLEDGMENTS

What a joy it has been to write these reflections about the gospel in *The Power Of The Gospel.* I'm so very thankful to the Lord for the idea and His guidance through the power of the Holy Spirit. I had so longed to glean the most important theological truths from Romans as a devotional photography journey as a companion to the quiet time experience of *The Proof of God's Amazing Love - A Quiet Time Experience.* I could have never written this book without the help of my beloved husband, David. Thank you, dear husband, for serving together with me in Quiet Time Ministries and for more than forty years together. Thank you to my precious family for their love and encouragement—David, Mother and Dad (both now with the Lord), Robert, Kayla, Linda, Christopher, Andy, Keegan, and James.

I am so very thankful over these many years for the Quiet Time Ministries team serving the Lord together with me—Kayla Branscum, Shirley Peters, Conni Hudson, Cindy Clark, Sandy Fallon, Paula Zillmer, Karen Darras Hawley, Kelly Wysard, Maurine Cromwell, and Cay Hough. Thank you to many dear friends who have offered such words of truth, encouragement, and hope that I have needed all along the way: Beverly Trupp, Conni Hudson, Cindy Clark, Andy Kotner Graybill, Jane Lyons, Julie Airis, Stefanie Kelly, Joe and Judy Patti, Betty Mann, Kelly Wysard, Jan Lupia, Barbara Waddell, Marilyn Meberg, and Vonette Bright.

Thank you to the Board of Directors of Quiet Time Ministries: David Martin, Conni Hudson, Andy Kotner Graybill, and Jane Lyons, for your faithfulness in this ministry. And thank you to all who have partnered with us both financially and prayerfully in Quiet Time Ministries. You have helped make possible this idea the Lord gave me so many years ago called Quiet Time Ministries and have allowed us to continue to spread God's Word to men and women throughout the world. I also want to thank those who have partnered financially with Quiet Time Ministries to sponsor myPhotoWalk photo shoots and purchase photographic equipment including my Nikon, Fuji and Sony cameras, lenses, tripods, and filters.

Thank you to my Bethel Seminary professors who gave me such a love for God's Word and helped me learn to study with excellence, especially Dr. Ronald Youngblood, Dr. Walt Wessel, Dr. James Smith, and Dr. Al Glenn.

Thank you to those who have encouraged me in devotional photography—especially Bill Fortney and His Light Friends, Laurie Rubin, Kevin Toohey, and Kathleen Reeder.

Thank you to Greg Johnson, my agent at WordServe Literary Agency, for all your support and encouragement.

Thank you to Friendship Church, and all the faithful women, pastors, and leaders I have had the privilege of serving with over the years in ministry. I am thankful for the beloved women I have had the opportunity to lead and pastor all these years. Thank you to all you amazing women in our online Bible study that meets on Thursday mornings — your love for God and His Word and your prayers are such a blessing in my life! A special thank you to all the groups worldwide who are drawing near to God in quiet time using the many quiet time studies and resources from Quiet Time Ministries.

Thank you to all those saints who have lived their lives with a passion for God and have encouraged me to love the Lord with all my heart and spend daily quiet time with Him. Finally, thank You, Lord, for leading and guiding me all the days of my life. To You be the glory.

MYPHOTOWALK

QUIET TIME MOMENTS

Devotional Photography to Refresh Your Heart

CATHERINE MARTIN

MYPHOTOWALK – QUIET TIME MOMENTS

MARTIN

Quiet Time Press

SAVORING GOD'S PROMISES OF HOPE MARTIN

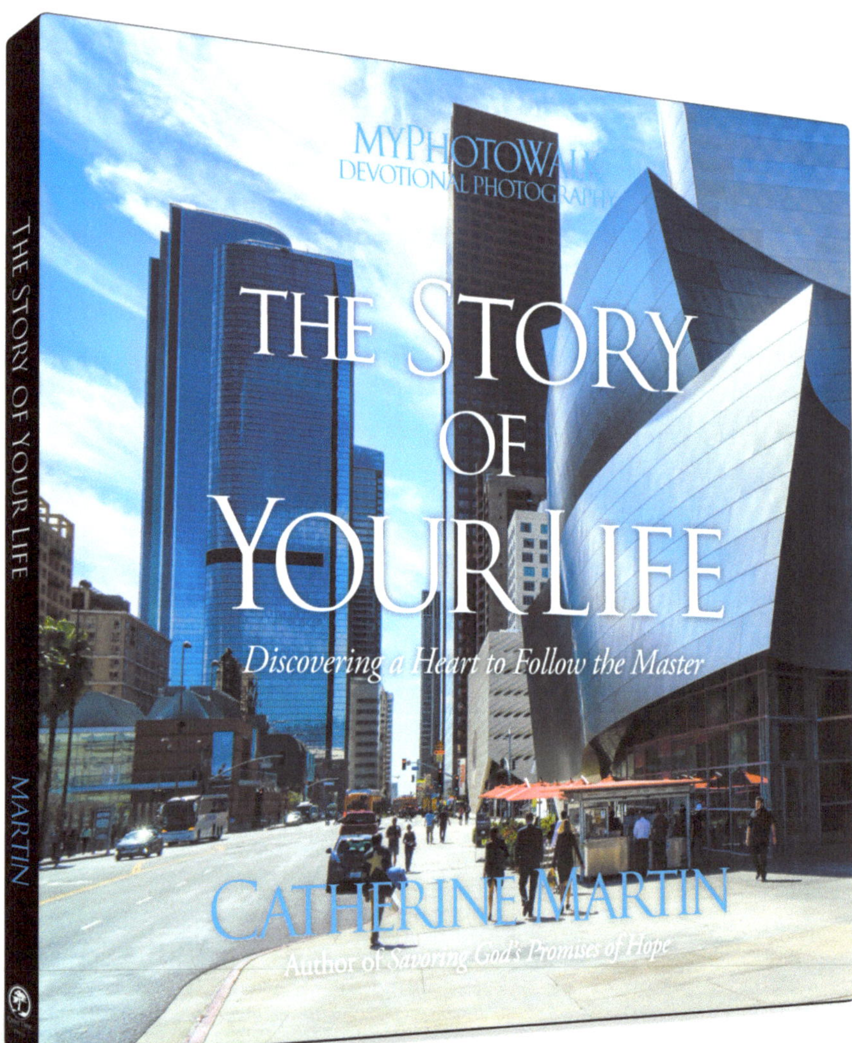
MYPHOTOWALK
DEVOTIONAL PHOTOGRAPHY
THE STORY OF YOUR LIFE
Discovering a Heart to Follow the Master
CATHERINE MARTIN
Author of Savoring God's Promises of Hope
THE STORY OF YOUR LIFE
MARTIN

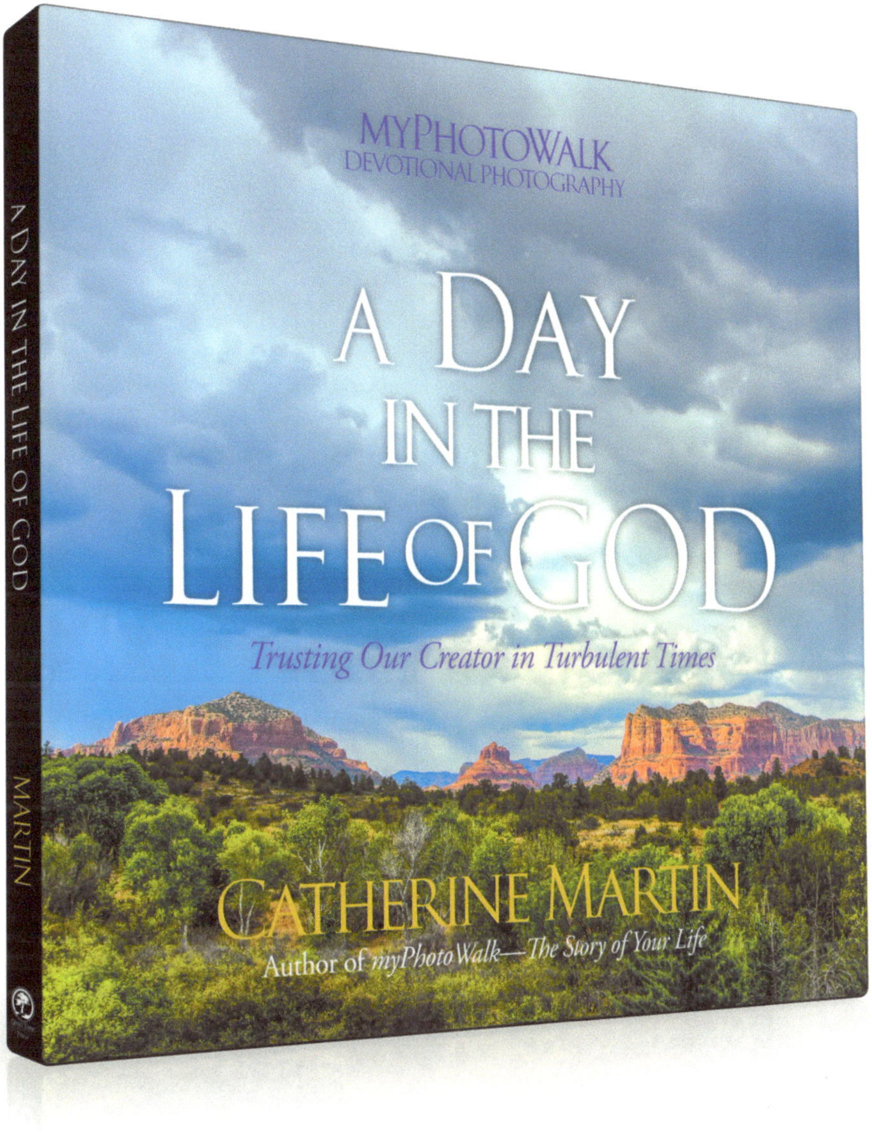

MYPHOTOWALK
DEVOTIONAL PHOTOGRAPHY

A DAY IN THE LIFE OF GOD

Trusting Our Creator in Turbulent Times

CATHERINE MARTIN

Author of *myPhotoWalk—The Story of Your Life*

A DAY IN THE LIFE OF GOD

MARTIN

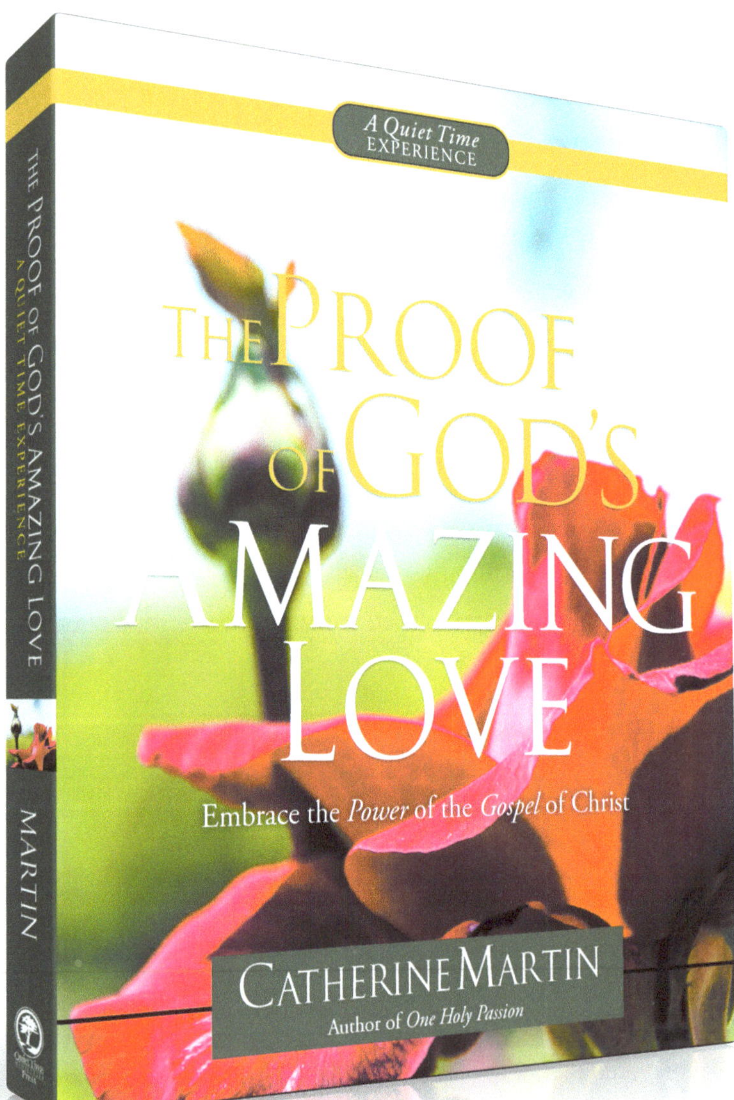
A Quiet Time EXPERIENCE
THE PROOF OF GOD'S AMAZING LOVE
Embrace the Power of the Gospel of Christ
CATHERINE MARTIN
Author of One Holy Passion
THE PROOF OF GOD'S AMAZING LOVE
A QUIET TIME EXPERIENCE
MARTIN

CATHERINE MARTIN

Author of *myPhotoWalk—The Story of Your Life*

THE CALLING

The *Story* of *Who You Are* and *Why You Are Here*

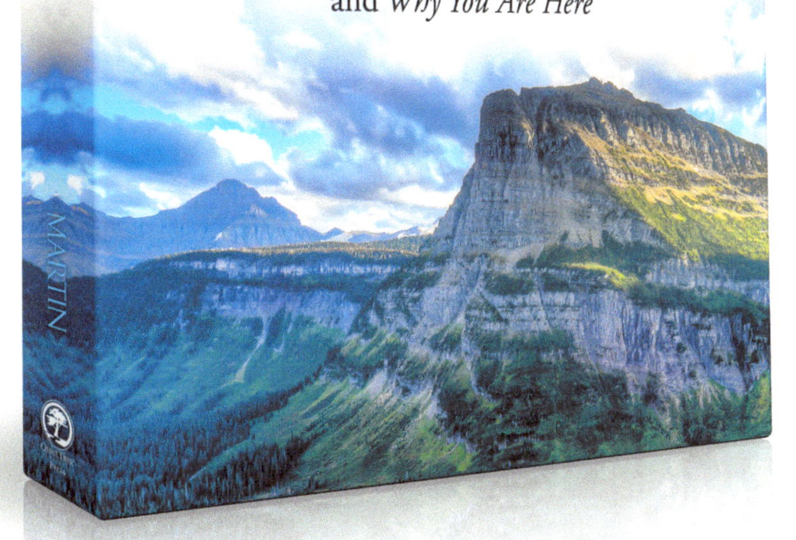

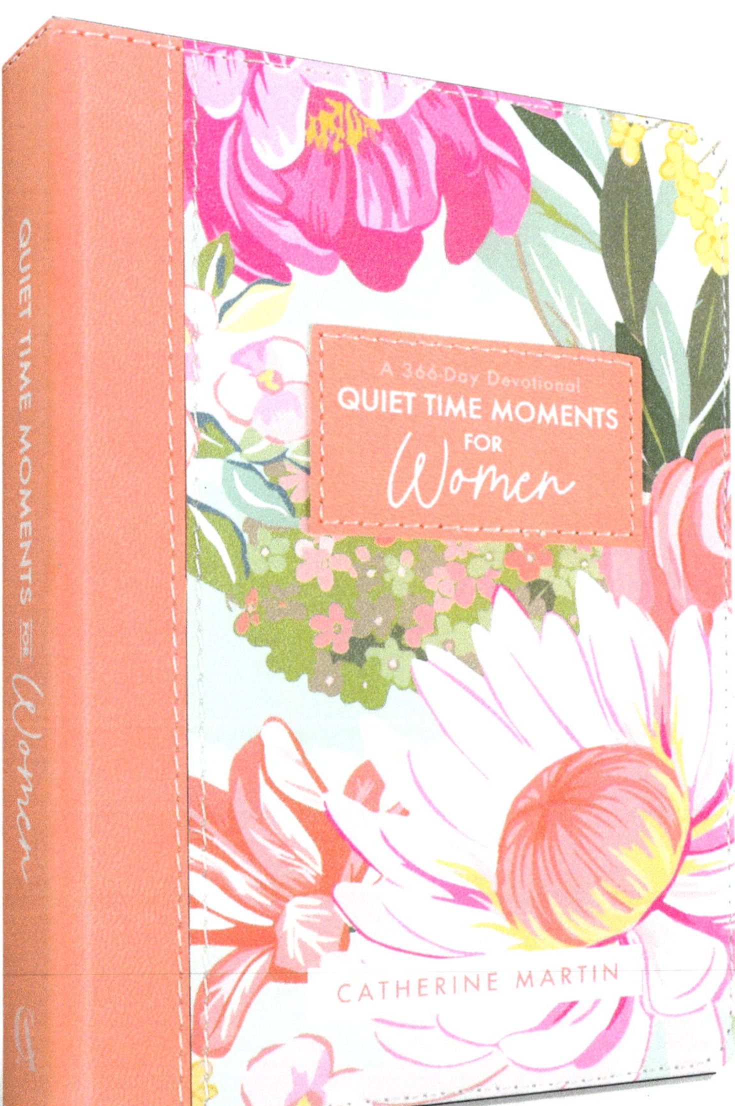

A 366-Day Devotional
QUIET TIME MOMENTS
FOR
Women
CATHERINE MARTIN
QUIET TIME MOMENTS FOR Women

www.ingramcontent.com/pod-product-compliance
Lightning Source LLC
LaVergne TN
LVHW071632100826
845154LV00008BA/135

* 9 7 8 1 7 3 7 5 7 4 7 1 2 *